To:

_____

From:

_____

Date:

_____

Promises from God for Purposeful Living

© 2006 Christian Art Gifts, RSA
    Christian Art Gifts Inc., IL, USA

First edition © 2006

Designed by Christian Art Gifts
Compiled by Lynette Douglas

ISBN 978-1-86920-589-8

Printed in China

07 08 09 10 11 12 13 14 15 16 – 11 10 9 8 7 6 5 4 3 2

PROMISES
FROM GOD
FOR
PURPOSEFUL
LIVING

christian
art gifts

Contents

Introduction

In him we were also chosen, having been predestined according to the plan of him who works out everything in conformity with the purpose of his will, in order that we, who were the first to hope in Christ, might be for the praise of his glory.

Ephesians 1:11-12 NIV

You have been chosen by God to live your life to His glory. He created you and filled you with potential. You need not do anything in your power for He has promised to equip you to live victoriously.

All you have to do is to trust Him completely to work in you through His Holy Spirit. A victorious life in union with Christ lies ahead of you. Filled with His mercy and compassion, you will be able to serve your fellowman faithfully.

Trust God's promises and you will be richly rewarded. In Him you will be blessed with peace. You can be certain that you have eternal life and that you are sanctified. Place your hope in God your Father. He will work out everything in your life with His glorious purpose in mind.

The LORD will give strength
to His people;
the LORD will bless
His people with peace.

~ Psalm 29:11, NKJV

Acceptance

For I am convinced that neither death
nor life ... nor anything in all creation,
will be able to separate us from the love
of God that is in Christ Jesus our Lord.
Romans 8:38-39 NIV

People all over the world, from rich to poor, from famous to unknown, from city dwellers to farmers, have one thing in common – they all want to belong, to be accepted and to be loved just as they are. "Accept me!" is the secret whisper of every heart.

The good news of the gospel is that God did accept you. He adopted you into His family, put the royal robe of welcome around your shoulders and led you to His banqueting table. He loved you so much that He did not want to live without you.

That is why He sent Jesus, His only begotten Son, to die so that you could live with Him forever. So rejoice in Him and live as a child of the Most High, loving Him and others because He first loved you.

Unconditional Acceptance

He chose us in Him before the foundation of the world, that we should be holy and without blame before Him in love, having predestined us to adoption as sons by Jesus Christ to Himself, according to the good pleasure of His will, to the praise of the glory of His grace, by which He made us accepted in the Beloved.

Ephesians 1:4-6 NKJV

For you are a people holy to the LORD your God. The LORD your God has chosen you out of all the peoples on the face of the earth to be his people, his treasured possession.

Deuteronomy 7:6 NIV

Know that the LORD, he is God! It is he who made us, and we are his; we are his people, and the sheep of his pasture.

Psalm 100:3 ESV

Because ye are sons, God hath sent forth the Spirit of his Son into your hearts, crying, "Abba, Father." Wherefore thou art no more a servant, but a son; and if a son, then an heir of God through Christ.

Galatians 4:6-7 KJV

"All that the Father gives me will come to me, and whoever comes to me I will never cast out."

John 6:37 ESV

For we are God's workmanship, created in Christ Jesus to do good works, which God prepared in advance for us to do.

Ephesians 2:10 NIV

But now thus saith the LORD that created thee, O Jacob, and he that formed thee, O Israel, Fear not: for I have redeemed thee, I have called thee by thy name; thou art mine.

Isaiah 43:1 KJV

The LORD hath appeared of old unto me, saying, "Yea, I have loved thee with an everlasting love: therefore with lovingkindness have I drawn thee."

Jeremiah 31:3 KJV

"Can a mother forget the baby at her breast and have no compassion on the child she has borne? Though she may forget, I will not forget you! See, I have engraved you on the palms of my hands."

Isaiah 49:15-16 NIV

God shows his love for us in that while we were still sinners, Christ died for us.

Romans 5:8 ESV

But now in Christ Jesus you
who once were far off have been
brought near by the blood of Christ.

Ephesians 2:13 NKJV

As many as received Him, to them He gave the right to become children of God, to those who believe in His name.

John 1:12 NKJV

So then you are no longer strangers and aliens, but you are fellow citizens with the saints and members of the household of God.

Ephesians 2:19 ESV

How great is the love the Father has lavished on us, that we should be called children of God! And that is what we are!

1 John 3:1 NIV

Whom He foreknew, He also
predestined to be conformed to
the image of His Son, that He might be
the firstborn among many brethren.

Romans 8:29 NKJV

BOLDNESS

The LORD is my light and my salvation –
whom shall I fear?
Psalm 27:1 NIV

Courage takes many forms. Our towns and cities are full of people who quietly struggle to exist day after day; they retain honesty and self-respect in the face of seemingly insurmountable problems.

Courage is needed when everything seems lost and all hope seems gone. The courageous person will persevere when others have given up in despair. Where does this courage come from?

The determination to overcome calls forth a very special kind of perseverance in the moment of suffering and testing. Real courage originates deep in man's innermost being. The true quality of man's courage is determined by what is hidden in his heart.

When your spirit is in harmony with the Holy Spirit of God, your life is filled with a holy strength that enables you to face life with courage and confidence. If Christ dwells in you, no fear can paralyze you.

Boldness
in Christ, our Hope

Though an host should encamp against me, my heart shall not fear: though war should rise against me, in this will I be confident. One thing have I desired of the LORD, that will I seek after; that I may dwell in the house of the LORD all the days of my life, to behold the beauty of the LORD, and to enquire in his temple.

Psalm 27:3-4 KJV

The wicked man flees though no one pursues, but the righteous are as bold as a lion.

Proverbs 28:1 NIV

So we may boldly say: "The Lord is my helper; I will not fear. What can man do to me?"

Hebrews 13:6 NKJV

Beloved, if our heart does not condemn us, we have confidence before God.

1 John 3:21 ESV

Wait for the LORD; be strong, and let your heart take courage; wait for the LORD!

Psalm 27:14 ESV

You shall not be terrified of them; for the LORD your God, the great and awesome God, is among you.

Deuteronomy 7:21 NKJV

"Have I not commanded you? Be strong and courageous. Do not be terrified; do not be discouraged, for the LORD your God will be with you wherever you go."

Joshua 1:9 NIV

"These things I have spoken unto you, that in me ye might have peace. In the world ye shall have tribulation: but be of good cheer; I have overcome the world."

John 16:33 KJV

For God has not given us a spirit of fear, but of power and of love and of a sound mind.

2 Timothy 1:7 NKJV

"Fear not, for I am with you; be not dismayed, for I am your God; I will strengthen you, I will help you, I will uphold you with my righteous right hand."

Isaiah 41:10 ESV

"When you pass through the waters, I will be with you; and when you pass through the rivers, they will not sweep over you. When you walk through the fire, you will not be burned; the flames will not set you ablaze. For I am the LORD, your God, the Holy One of Israel."

Isaiah 43:2-3 NIV

Be of good courage, and he shall strengthen your heart, all ye that hope in the LORD.

Psalm 31:24 KJV

He gives strength to the weary and increases the power of the weak.

Isaiah 40:29 NIV

In all these things we are more than conquerors through him that loved us.

Romans 8:37 KJV

I can do all things through Christ who strengthens me.

Philippians 4:13 NKJV

CHRISTIAN FELLOWSHIP

They are to do good, to be rich in good works,
to be generous and ready to share.

1 Timothy 6:18 ESV

We praise God that in the midst of the chaos in our world there is a powerful core of believers whose first, last and only love is the risen Christ. Their doctrines and spiritual traditions might seem irreconcilable; they might feel isolated because of cultural differences, but in every heart the same love for the Lord Jesus Christ burns brightly. This true love forms the basis of the triumphant church of Christ on earth.

When Christians care for the needy in the community, it is a practical demonstration of love. Christian love is inspired by the unselfish love of Christ and that distinguishes it from social welfare.

Those who really love Christ rise above all differences and are free from all forms of pettiness and narrow-mindedness. They no longer judge fellow Christians by their doctrines, but accept them in love.

Nurturing
Christian Fellowship

That which we have seen and heard declare we unto you, that ye also may have fellowship with us: and truly our fellowship is with the Father, and with his Son Jesus Christ.

1 John 1:3 KJV

All who believed were together and had all things in common. And they were selling their possessions and belongings and distributing the proceeds to all, as any had need. And day by day, attending the temple together and breaking bread in their homes, they received their food with glad and generous hearts, praising God and having favor with all the people. And the Lord added to their number day by day those who were being saved.

Acts 2:44-47 ESV

Let us consider how we may spur one another on toward love and good deeds. Let us not give up meeting together, as some are in the habit of doing, but let us encourage one another – and all the more as you see the Day approaching.

Hebrews 10:24-25 NIV

So then, as we have opportunity, let us do good to everyone, and especially to those who are of the household of faith.

Galatians 6:10 ESV

LORD, who may dwell in your sanctuary?
Who may live on your holy hill?
He whose walk is blameless and who does
what is righteous, who speaks the truth
from his heart and has no slander on his
tongue, who does his neighbor no wrong
and casts no slur on his fellowman.

Psalm 15:1-3 NIV

If you really fulfill the royal law according to the Scripture, "You shall love your neighbor as yourself," you do well.

James 2:8 NKJV

Owe no man any thing, but to love one
another: for he that loveth another hath
fulfilled the law. For this, Thou shalt not
commit adultery, Thou shalt not kill, Thou
shalt not steal, Thou shalt not bear false
witness, Thou shalt not covet; and if there be
any other commandment, it is briefly
comprehended in this saying, namely,
Thou shalt love thy neighbour as thyself.
Love worketh no ill to his neighbour:
therefore love is the fulfilling of the law.

Romans 13:8-10 KJV

Jesus answered him, "The first of all the commandments is: 'Hear, O Israel, the Lord our God, the Lord is one. And you shall love the Lord your God with all your heart, with all your soul, with all your mind, and with all your strength.' This is the first commandment. And the second, like it, is this: 'You shall love your neighbor as yourself.' There is no other commandment greater than these."

Mark 12:29-31 NKJV

Therefore, putting away lying, "Let each one of you speak truth with his neighbor," for we are members of one another.

Ephesians 4:25 NKJV

Let each of us please his neighbor for his good, leading to edification.

Romans 15:2 NKJV

Love must be sincere. Hate what is evil; cling to what is good. Be devoted to one another in brotherly love. Honor one another above yourselves. Share with God's people who are in need. Rejoice with those who rejoice; mourn with those who mourn. Live in harmony with one another.

Romans 12:9-10, 13, 15-16 NIV

COMFORT

He will wipe away every tear from
their eyes, and death shall be no more.
Revelation 21:4 ESV

Some people do not believe that Jesus understands human problems. They see the Lord as Someone far removed from our everyday lives and who is only interested in matters of universal importance. Such an attitude reveals a complete misunderstanding of God and His loving concern for the world He created and the people for whom His Son died.

Although God is King of kings and Lord of lords, we must never forget that Jesus is not only our Master, but also our Friend. Because He lived, suffered and died as a human being, He understands human problems and emotions. He also endured suffering, disappointment, sorrow and joy.

The Savior is waiting for you to invite Him to share your life with Him. Open your heart to Him and He will help you in whatever circumstances you may find yourself in.

Through Christ
We are Comforted

Therefore we do not lose heart. Even though our outward man is perishing, yet the inward man is being renewed day by day. For our light affliction, which is but for a moment, is working for us a far more exceeding and eternal weight of glory, while we do not look at the things which are seen, but at the things which are not seen. For the things which are seen are temporary, but the things which are not seen are eternal.

2 Corinthians 4:16-18 NKJV

Yea, though I walk through the valley
of the shadow of death, I will fear no evil:
for thou art with me; thy rod
and thy staff they comfort me.

Psalm 23:4 KJV

"Blessed are those who mourn: for they shall be comforted."

Matthew 5:4 KJV

"I will not leave you comfortless:
I will come to you."

John 14:18 KJV

This I call to mind, and therefore I have hope:
The steadfast love of the LORD never ceases;
his mercies never come to an end.

Lamentations 3:21-22 ESV

Who shall separate us from the love of
Christ? Shall tribulation, or distress, or
persecution, or famine, or nakedness, or
danger, or sword? As it is written, "For your
sake we are being killed all the day long;
we are regarded as sheep to be slaughtered."
No, in all these things we are more than
conquerors through him who loved us.
For I am sure that neither death nor life, nor
angels nor rulers, nor things present nor
things to come, nor powers, nor height nor
depth, nor anything else in all creation,
will be able to separate us from the
love of God in Christ Jesus our Lord.

Romans 8:35-39 ESV

The LORD is close to the brokenhearted and
saves those who are crushed in spirit.

Psalm 34:18 NIV

The eternal God is your refuge,
and underneath are the everlasting arms.

Deuteronomy 33:27 NKJV

"I will not forget you! See, I have engraved you on the palms of my hands; your walls are ever before me."

Isaiah 49:15-16 NIV

"I will pray the Father, and he shall give you another Comforter, that he may abide with you for ever."

John 14:16 KJV

"Comfort, comfort my people," says your God. "Speak tenderly to Jerusalem, and proclaim to her that her hard service has been completed, that her sin has been paid for."

Isaiah 40:1-2 NIV

Surely He has borne our griefs and carried our sorrows; yet we esteemed Him stricken, smitten by God, and afflicted.

Isaiah 53:4 NKJV

Praise be to the God and Father of our Lord Jesus Christ, the Father of compassion and the God of all comfort, who comforts us in all our troubles, so that we can comfort those in any trouble with the comfort we ourselves have received from God.

2 Corinthians 1:3-4 NIV

Encouragement

Let the morning bring me word of your
unfailing love, for I have put my trust in you.

Psalm 143:8 NIV

Most of us have experienced adverse circumstances that dramatically affected us, as well as those we love. How often has your world been disrupted by serious illness, death, failure or financial disaster?

Nevertheless, you have the assurance of God's love for you. However despondent you may be about unexpected events and circumstances that cause you great anxiety, never lose sight of the fact that Jesus loves you with an unfailing, eternal and perfect love. He will ease your burden if you turn to Him in prayer and faith. He will allay your fears and concerns and give you His Holy Spirit to comfort and lead you.

Regardless of circumstances, or how dark the future may seem, if you take God at His Word and listen to His promises, you will enjoy His blessings as well as His peace that drives out all fear (1 John 4:18).

Encouragement to Endure

The LORD is my light and my salvation; whom shall I fear? The LORD is the strength of my life; of whom shall I be afraid?

Psalm 27:1 KJV

God is our refuge and strength, an ever-present help in trouble. Therefore we will not fear, though the earth give way and the mountains fall into the heart of the sea.

Psalm 46:1-2 NIV

Yet the LORD will command his lovingkindness in the daytime, and in the night his song shall be with me, and my prayer unto the God of my life.

Psalm 42:8 KJV

Yet the LORD longs to be gracious to you; he rises to show you compassion. For the LORD is a God of justice. Blessed are all who wait for him!

Isaiah 30:18 NIV

For you have need of endurance, so that after you have done the will of God, you may receive the promise.

Hebrews 10:36 NKJV

In all my prayers for all of you, I always pray with joy because of your partnership in the gospel from the first day until now, being confident of this, that he who began a good work in you will carry it on to completion until the day of Christ Jesus.

Philippians 1:4-6 NIV

Count it all joy, my brothers, when you meet trials of various kinds, for you know that the testing of your faith produces steadfastness. And let steadfastness have its full effect, that you may be perfect and complete, lacking in nothing.

James 1:2-4 ESV

In this you rejoice, though now for a little while, if necessary, you have been grieved by various trials, so that the tested genuineness of your faith – more precious than gold that perishes though it is tested by fire – may be found to result in praise and glory and honor at the revelation of Jesus Christ.

1 Peter 1:6-7 ESV

Let the morning bring me word of your unfailing love, for I have put my trust in you. Show me the way I should go, for to you I lift up my soul.

Psalm 143:8 NIV

And not only that, but we also glory in tribulations, knowing that tribulation produces perseverance; and perseverance, character; and character, hope. Now hope does not disappoint, because the love of God has been poured out in our hearts by the Holy Spirit who was given to us.

Romans 5:3-5 NKJV

But rejoice, inasmuch as ye are
partakers of Christ's sufferings; that,
when his glory shall be revealed,
ye may be glad also with exceeding joy.

1 Peter 4:13 KJV

There hath no temptation taken you but such as is common to man: but God is faithful, who will not suffer you to be tempted above that ye are able; but will with the temptation also make a way to escape, that ye may be able to bear it.

1 Corinthians 10:13 KJV

Why are you cast down, O my soul?
And why are you disquieted within me?
Hope in God; For I shall yet praise Him,
the help of my countenance and my God.

Psalm 42:11 NKJV

ETERNAL LIFE

*He who has the Son has life; he who does
not have the Son of God does not have life.*

1 John 5:12 NIV

Many people often sigh and complain that there is nothing to live for. However, God's promise to you in Jesus Christ is that He will give you life in abundance! There are no limitations to the quality of life that Christ offers you.

Refresh your thinking by studying the Word of God; renew your spirit in the time you spend in prayer and meditation. Then you will discover a new purpose, a new energy and a new joy in your life.

Enrich your own life and the lives of others by having the same attitude as Jesus Christ. The Holy Spirit will guide you and give purpose and direction to your life. As you obey Him and live to His glory, the rich harvest of spiritual fruit will become visible in your life. You will see every day as a gift from God's hand and use every opportunity to live the eternal life here and now.

THE GIFT OF ETERNAL LIFE

If ye then be risen with Christ, seek those things which are above, where Christ sitteth on the right hand of God. Set your affection on things above, not on things on the earth. For ye are dead, and your life is hid with Christ in God. When Christ, who is our life, shall appear, then shall ye also appear with him in glory.

Colossians 3:1-4 KJV

You have come to Mount Zion,
to the heavenly Jerusalem, the city
of the living God. You have come to
thousands upon thousands of angels in
joyful assembly, to the church of the
firstborn, whose names are written in heaven.
You have come to God, the judge of all men, to
the spirits of righteous men made perfect, to
Jesus the mediator of a new covenant,
and to the sprinkled blood that speaks
a better word than the blood of Abel.

Hebrews 12:22-24 NIV

With long life will I satisfy him, and shew him my salvation.

Psalm 91:16 KJV

Jesus spoke these words, lifted up His eyes to heaven, and said: "Father, the hour has come. Glorify Your Son, that Your Son also may glorify You, as You have given Him authority over all flesh, that He should give eternal life to as many as You have given Him. And this is eternal life, that they may know You, the only true God, and Jesus Christ whom You have sent."

John 17:1-3 NKJV

Blessed be the God and Father of our Lord Jesus Christ! According to his great mercy, he has caused us to be born again to a living hope through the resurrection of Jesus Christ from the dead.

1 Peter 1:3 ESV

He will render to each one according to his works: to those who by patience in well-doing seek for glory and honor and immortality, he will give eternal life.

Romans 2:6-7 ESV

God raised us up with Christ and seated us with him in the heavenly realms in Christ Jesus, in order that in the coming ages he might show the incomparable riches of his grace, expressed in his kindness to us in Christ Jesus.

Ephesians 2:6-7 NIV

"For God so loved the world, that he gave his only begotten Son, that whosoever believeth in him should not perish, but have everlasting life. For God sent not his Son into the world to condemn the world; but that the world through him might be saved."

John 3:16-17 KJV

"But whosoever drinketh of the water that I shall give him shall never thirst; but the water that I shall give him shall be in him a well of water springing up into everlasting life."

John 4:14 KJV

"He who believes in the Son has everlasting life; and he who does not believe the Son shall not see life, but the wrath of God abides on him."

John 3:36 NKJV

"I have come that they may have life, and that they may have it more abundantly."

John 10:10 NKJV

"My sheep listen to my voice; I know them, and they follow me. I give them eternal life, and they shall never perish; no one can snatch them out of my hand."

John 10:27-28 NIV

FAITHFULNESS

*"Be faithful, even to the point of death,
and I will give you the crown of life."*

Revelation 2:10 NIV

Christ requires His followers to be faithful. He Himself demonstrated faithfulness when He sacrificed His life on the cross. When Christ asks us to be faithful to death, He also promises us a divine and royal reward: eternal life!

It is easy to be faithful when life is exciting and you are in the spotlight, but you also need to be faithful when the monotonous routine of your everyday duties begins to wear you down. Be faithful when no one sees you – because God sees you.

Be faithful to what is most noble in yourself. Shakespeare said, "To thine own self be true, and it must follow, as the night the day, thou canst not then be false to any man."

Above all, you should be faithful to God. He is the foundation and the Source of all that is good in your life. Without Him, life has no meaning.

Forever Faithful

Know therefore that the LORD your God is God; he is the faithful God, keeping his covenant of love to a thousand generations of those who love him and keep his commands.

Deuteronomy 7:9 NIV

Most men will proclaim every one his own goodness: but a faithful man who can find?

Proverbs 20:6 KJV

Because of the LORD's great love we are not consumed, for his compassions never fail. They are new every morning; great is your faithfulness.

Lamentations 3:22-23 NIV

His lord said to him, "Well done, good and faithful servant; you were faithful over a few things, I will make you ruler over many things. Enter into the joy of your lord."

Matthew 25:21 NKJV

The Lord is faithful, and he will strengthen and protect you from the evil one.

2 Thessalonians 3:3 NIV

These shall make war with the Lamb, and the Lamb shall overcome them: for he is Lord of lords, and King of kings: and they that are with him are called, and chosen, and faithful.

Revelation 17:14 KJV

"Whoever can be trusted with very little can also be trusted with much."
Luke 16:10 NIV

No temptation has overtaken you that is not common to man. God is faithful, and he will not let you be tempted beyond your ability, but with the temptation he will also provide the way of escape, that you may be able to endure it.

1 Corinthians 10:13 ESV

If we are faithless, he remains faithful –
for he cannot deny himself.
2 Timothy 2:13 ESV

Let us hold fast the confession of our hope without wavering, for He who promised is faithful.

Hebrews 10:23 NKJV

Your mercy, O LORD, is in the heavens;
Your faithfulness reaches to the clouds.
Psalm 36:5 NKJV

God is faithful, by whom ye were called unto the fellowship of his Son Jesus Christ our Lord.

1 Corinthians 1:9 KJV

God is not man, that He should lie,
nor a son of man, that He should repent.
Has He said, and will He not do? Or has
He spoken, and will He not make it good?

Numbers 23:19 NKJV

From the east I summon a bird of prey; from a far-off land, a man to fulfill my purpose. What I have said, that will I bring about; what I have planned, that will I do.

Isaiah 46:11 NIV

Therefore let those who suffer according
to God's will entrust their souls
to a faithful Creator while doing good.

1 Peter 4:19 ESV

It is good to give thanks to the LORD, to sing praises to your name, O Most High; to declare your steadfast love in the morning and your faithfulness by night.

Psalm 92:1-2 ESV

FAVOR

Give thanks to the LORD, for he is good.
His love endures forever.

Psalm 136:1 NIV

When talking about the good life, we do not usually begin by focusing on "strength in the Lord." However, that is exactly what the Psalmist does in Psalm 84 when he says, "They go from strength to strength."

Instead, we rather tend to focus on our happy families, comfortable homes, world travels or fulfilling careers. None of these is wrong in itself, but if your thoughts about the good life exclude God, they are indeed wrong. The Psalmist reminds himself that to worship God is far better than to enjoy a good life in the company of people. He knows that God fully understands what the good life is and that He will bless His obedient children with abundant life.

What a wonderful God we worship! He blesses and rewards those who faithfully follow Him. Thank God for the blessings that you have received from Him.

Finding Favor in God's Eyes

"I will turn to you and make you fruitful and multiply you and will confirm my covenant with you."

Leviticus 26:9 ESV

May the LORD bless his land with the precious dew from heaven above and with the deep waters that lie below; with the best the sun brings forth and the finest the moon can yield; with the choicest gifts of the ancient mountains and the fruitfulness of the everlasting hills; with the best gifts of the earth and its fullness and the favor of him who dwelt in the burning bush. Let all these rest on the head of Joseph, on the brow of the prince among his brothers.

Deuteronomy 33:13-16 NIV

Go, eat your food with gladness, and drink your wine with a joyful heart, for it is now that God favors what you do.

Ecclesiastes 9:7 NIV

May the favor of the Lord our God rest upon us; establish the work of our hands for us – yes, establish the work of our hands.

Psalm 90:17 NIV

The Lord was with him; he showed him kindness and granted him favor in the eyes of the prison warden.

Genesis 39:21 NIV

He shall pray to God, and He will delight
in him, He shall see His face with joy;
for He restores to man His righteousness.

Job 33:26 NKJV

"O Lord, let your ear be attentive to the prayer of this your servant and to the prayer of your servants who delight in revering your name. Give your servant success today by granting him favor in the presence of this man."

Nehemiah 1:11 NIV

For surely, O Lord, you bless
the righteous; you surround them
with your favor as with a shield.

Psalm 5:12 NIV

My prayer is to you, O Lord. At an acceptable time, O God, in the abundance of your steadfast love answer me in your saving faithfulness.

Psalm 69:13 ESV

For the Lord God is a sun and shield: the Lord will give grace and glory: no good thing will he withhold from them that walk uprightly.

Psalm 84:11 KJV

Let not mercy and truth forsake you;
bind them around your neck, write them on
the tablet of your heart, and so find favor and
high esteem in the sight of God and man.

Proverbs 3:3-4 NKJV

The Spirit of the Lord God is upon me; because the Lord hath anointed me to preach good tidings unto the meek; he hath sent me to bind up the brokenhearted, to proclaim liberty to the captives, and the opening of the prison to them that are bound.

Isaiah 61:1 KJV

For He says: "In an acceptable time I have
heard you, and in the day of salvation I have
helped you." Behold, now is the accepted
time; behold, now is the day of salvation.

2 Corinthians 6:2 NKJV

"Glory to God in the highest, and on earth peace to men on whom his favor rests."

Luke 2:14 NIV

FRIENDS

If one falls down, his friend can help him up.
But pity the man who falls
and has no one to help him up.

Ecclesiastes 4:10 NIV

A friend is someone you can turn to without hesitation when you go through hard times and who sincerely rejoices when things go well for you. He gives you advice when you are worried and encouragement when you need to solve a problem. You can lean on him when your heart is breaking, yet he never exploits your vulnerability.

You can cry on his shoulder when you are sad and laugh with him when you are cheerful. He marvels at your good qualities and loves you in spite of your weaknesses.

He is proud when you achieve your goals, but not ashamed of you when you fail. He will speak the truth in love, and you can tell him the truth without fear of offending him.

He will not hesitate to prove his friendship, even at the risk of it being abused. He offers help without expecting something in return.

Faithful Friends

How good and pleasant it is when brothers live together in unity! It is like precious oil poured on the head, running down on the beard, running down on Aaron's beard, down upon the collar of his robes. It is as if the dew of Hermon were falling on Mount Zion. For there the Lord bestows his blessing, even life forevermore.

Psalm 133 NIV

Be kind and compassionate to
one another, forgiving each other,
just as in Christ God forgave you.

Ephesians 4:32 NIV

I thank my God every time I remember you. In all my prayers for all of you, I always pray with joy because of your partnership in the gospel from the first day until now.

Philippians 1:3-5 NIV

A new commandment I give to you,
that you love one another: just as I have
loved you, you also are to love one another.
By this all people will know that you are my
disciples, if you have love for one another.

John 13:34-35 ESV

I thank my God always on your behalf, for the grace of God which is given you by Jesus Christ.

1 Corinthians 1:4 KJV

Beloved, let us love one another,
for love is of God; and everyone who
loves is born of God and knows God.

1 John 4:7 NKJV

Carry each other's burdens, and in this way you will fulfill the law of Christ.

Galatians 6:2 NIV

Therefore if there is any consolation in Christ,
if any comfort of love, if any fellowship
of the Spirit, if any affection and mercy, fulfill
my joy by being like-minded, having the
same love, being of one accord, of one mind.

Philippians 2:1-2 NKJV

Two are better than one, because they have a good reward for their labor. For if they fall, one will lift up his companion.

Ecclesiastes 4:9-10 NKJV

Oil and perfume make the heart glad,
and the sweetness of a friend
comes from his earnest counsel.

Proverbs 27:9 ESV

Beloved, if God so loved us, we ought also to love one another. No man hath seen God at any time. If we love one another, God dwelleth in us, and his love is perfected in us. Hereby know we that we dwell in him, and he in us, because he hath given us of his Spirit.

1 John 4:11-13 KJV

Therefore encourage one another and build one another up, just as you are doing.

1 Thessalonians 5:11 ESV

I am a friend to all who fear you, to all who follow your precepts.

Psalm 119:63 NIV

May God be gracious to us and bless us and make his face shine upon us.

Psalm 67:1 NIV

My purpose is that they may be encouraged in heart and united in love, so that they may have the full riches of complete understanding, in order that they may know the mystery of God, namely, Christ.

Colossians 2:2 NIV

FRUITFULNESS

"A good tree does not bear bad fruit,
nor does a bad tree bear good fruit.
For every tree is known by its own fruit."

Luke 6:43-44 NKJV

God's grace, together with our surrender to His love, results in our being fruit-bearing disciples.

We were chosen to serve with joy, however difficult the task. Our lives and work for the Master should radiate joy, because we are privileged to be His children.

We were chosen to serve in love. Without love, we cannot be ambassadors of the Source of all true love. Love gives us a passion for souls and keeps us from competing with one another for petty honor.

Since Christ calls us His friends, we must guard against becoming like the elder brother in the parable of the lost son. This attitude so easily creeps into our prayer lives, Bible study, worship and relationships. Our service and fruitfulness should reveal what is most noble in our lives. The world should be able to see that we are workers in God's vineyard.

What the Word says about Fruitfulness

Live a life worthy of the Lord and please him in every way: bearing fruit in every good work, growing in the knowledge of God, being strengthened with all power according to his glorious might so that you may have great endurance and patience.

Colossians 1:10-11 NIV

The work of righteousness shall
be peace; and the effect of righteousness
quietness and assurance for ever.

Isaiah 32:17 KJV

The righteous flourish like the palm tree and grow like a cedar in Lebanon. They are planted in the house of the LORD; they flourish in the courts of our God. They still bear fruit in old age; they are ever full of sap and green.

Psalm 92:12-14 ESV

The fruit of the Spirit is love, joy,
peace, patience, kindness, goodness,
faithfulness, gentleness and self-control.
Against such things there is no law.

Galatians 5:22-23 NIV

For the fruit of light is found in all that is good and right and true.

Ephesians 5:9 ESV

Now the fruit of righteousness is sown
in peace by those who make peace.

James 3:18 NKJV

Sow for yourselves righteousness, reap the fruit of unfailing love, and break up your unplowed ground; for it is time to seek the LORD, until he comes and showers righteousness on you.

Hosea 10:12 NIV

Blessed is the man who walks not
in the counsel of the ungodly, nor stands in
the path of sinners, nor sits in the seat of
the scornful; but his delight is in the law of
the LORD, and in His law he meditates day
and night. He shall be like a tree planted
by the rivers of water, that brings forth its
fruit in its season, whose leaf shall not
wither; and whatever he does shall prosper.

Psalm 1:1-3 NKJV

"I am the vine, ye are the branches: He that abideth in me, and I in him, the same bringeth forth much fruit."

John 15:5 KJV

Tell the righteous it will be well with them,
for they will enjoy the fruit of their deeds.

Isaiah 3:10 NIV

Blessed is everyone who fears the LORD,
who walks in his ways! You shall eat the
fruit of the labor of you hands; you shall
be blessed, and it shall be well with you.

Psalm 128:1-2 ESV

The fruit of the righteous is a tree of life;
and he that winneth souls is wise.

Proverbs 11:30 KJV

From the fruit of his mouth
a man is satisfied with good.

Proverbs 12:14 ESV

The LORD will guide you continually and
satisfy your desire in scorched places and
make your bones strong; and you shall be
like a watered garden, like a spring of water,
whose waters do not fail.

Isaiah 58:11 ESV

The trees of the field will yield their
fruit and the ground will yield its crops;
the people will be secure in their land.
They will know that I am the LORD.

Ezekiel 34:27 NIV

Because your love is better than life,
my lips will glorify you. I will
praise you as long as I live, and in
your name I will lift up my hands.

~ Psalm 63:3-4, NIV

THE FUTURE

All the days ordained for me were written
in your book before one of them came to be.

Psalm 139:16 NIV

We usually view the future with mixed feelings. Will the failures of the past be repeated and will monotony bog us down?

What the future holds depends largely on you. You could sidestep its challenges and continue in the same rut that you have been in, or you could grasp new opportunities and develop a new approach to life.

You could approach the future as you did the past: wanting to do better, but convinced that before long you will experience the same unfulfilled expectations and doleful failures of yesterday. You could meet the future with the full realization of who you are in Christ and with the conviction that you serve a wonderful God who desires only victory for you.

God offers you eternal life and the privilege of being His child. If you trust in Jesus Christ, the future will not hold defeat or failure for you.

HOPE FOR THE FUTURE

If that is how God clothes the grass of the field, which is here today and tomorrow is thrown into the fire, will he not much more clothe you, O you of little faith? So do not worry, saying, "What shall we eat?" or "What shall we drink?" or "What shall we wear?" For the pagans run after all these things, and your heavenly Father knows that you need them. But seek first his kingdom and his righteousness, and all these things will be given to you as well. Therefore do not worry about tomorrow, for tomorrow will worry about itself. Each day has enough trouble of its own.

Matthew 6:30-34 NIV

A heart at peace gives life to
the body, but envy rots the bones.
Proverbs 14:30 NIV

Let us not grow weary while doing good, for in due season we shall reap if we do not lose heart. Therefore, as we have opportunity, let us do good to all, especially to those who are of the household of faith.

Galatians 6:9-10 NKJV

Do not let your heart envy sinners, but always be zealous for the fear of the Lord. There is surely a future hope for you, and your hope will not be cut off.

Proverbs 23:17-18 niv

Many are the plans in the mind of a man,
but it is the purpose of the Lord that will stand.

Proverbs 19:21 esv

May he give you the desire of your heart and make all your plans succeed.

Psalm 20:4 niv

The counsel of the Lord standeth for ever,
the thoughts of his heart to all generations.

Psalm 33:11 kjv

Now listen, you who say, "Today or tomorrow we will go to this or that city, spend a year there, carry on business and make money." Why, you do not even know what will happen tomorrow. What is your life? You are a mist that appears for a little while and then vanishes. Instead, you ought to say, "If it is the Lord's will, we will live and do this or that."

James 4:13-15 niv

The LORD will perfect that which concerns me; your mercy, O LORD, endures forever; do not forsake the works of Your hands.

Psalm 138:8 NKJV

I make known the end from the beginning, from ancient times, what is still to come. I say: My purpose will stand, and I will do all that I please.

Isaiah 46:10 NIV

Mark the blameless man, and observe the upright; for the future of that man is peace.

Psalm 37:37 NKJV

"For I know the plans I have for you," declares the LORD, "plans to prosper you and not to harm you, plans to give you hope and a future."

Jeremiah 29:11 NIV

I will cry unto God most high; unto God that performeth all things for me.

Psalm 57:2 KJV

Do not boast about tomorrow, for you do not know what a day may bring.

Proverbs 27:1 ESV

GENEROSITY

*Everything comes from you, and we have
given you only what comes from your hand.*

1 Chronicles 29:14 NIV

God gave us the great gift of His Son
and when gifts are given with joy, their
value is enhanced. Every Christian is called
to be a giver. The Holy Spirit teaches you
not to withhold anything that will bless
your neighbor. Your purpose in life is to be
a blessing to others.

When you give someone a gift, pray that
God will bless the receiver. Money or possessions are not the most important gifts
that you can give. You should develop your
character and personality to God's glory
and use it in the service of others. The world
desperately needs love and kindess. When
you give of yourself, you give the most
generous gift of all.

Do not calculate whether you will profit
from a gift you have given. God gives freely
and you and I should do the same.

Giving and Generosity

I was young and now I am old, yet I have never seen the righteous forsaken or their children begging bread. They are always generous and lend freely; their children will be blessed.

Psalm 37:25-26 NIV

Blessed is he that considereth the poor:
the LORD will deliver him in time of trouble.

Psalm 41:1 KJV

One man gives freely, yet gains even more; another withholds unduly, but comes to poverty. A generous man will prosper; he who refreshes others will himself be refreshed.

Proverbs 11:24-25 NIV

Each man should give what he has
decided in his heart to give, not reluctantly
or under compulsion, for God loves a
cheerful giver. And God is able to make
all grace abound to you, so that in all
things at all times, having all that you need,
you will abound in every good work.

2 Corinthians 9:7-8 NIV

"Give, and it will be given to you. Good measure, pressed down, shaken together, running over, will be put into your lap. For with the measure you use it will be measured to you."

Luke 6:38 ESV

"You must support the weak. And remember the words of the Lord Jesus, that He said, 'It is more blessed to give than to receive.'"

Acts 20:35 NKJV

Therefore, as ye abound in every thing, in faith, and utterance, and knowledge, and in all diligence, and in your love to us, see that ye abound in this grace also.

2 Corinthians 8:7 KJV

For you know the grace of our Lord Jesus Christ, that though he was rich, yet for your sakes he became poor, so that you through his poverty might become rich.

2 Corinthians 8:9 NIV

He who supplies seed to the sower and bread for food will supply and multiply your seed for sowing and increase the harvest of your righteousness.

2 Corinthians 9:10 ESV

You will be made rich in every way so that you can be generous on every occasion, and through us your generosity will result in thanksgiving to God.

2 Corinthians 9:11 NIV

"And you shall remember the LORD your God, for it is He who gives you power to get wealth, that He may establish His covenant which He swore to your fathers, as it is this day."

Deuteronomy 8:18 NKJV

Honor the LORD with your wealth and with the firstfruits of all your produce; then your barns will be filled with plenty, and your vats will be bursting with wine.

Proverbs 3:9-10 ESV

God is not unjust; he will not forget your work and the love you have shown him as you have helped his people and continue to help them.

Hebrews 6:10 NIV

He who has pity on the poor lends to the LORD, and He will pay back what he has given.

Proverbs 19:17 NKJV

GOD'S LOVE

This is how God showed his love among us:
He sent his one and only Son into
the world that we might live through him.

1 John 4:9 NIV

God has no favorites. Whether you are an ordinary person or a celebrity, a business leader or a blue collar worker, in God's eyes you are special because He created you, you are His child and He loves you.

Many people torture themselves with the thought that they have disappointed God, or that they have neglected their spiritual lives and that God is angry with them.

Look at how Jesus treated people when He was in the world and you will see that everyone received the same love, care, grace and compassion. The living Christ reached out to both the worthy and the unworthy. He forgave His enemies, even though they nailed Him to a cross.

Do not give in to feelings of inferiority. He chose you and saved you. You belong to God; you are His child and He loves you dearly.

God's Divine Love

How excellent is thy lovingkindness, O God!
Therefore the children of men put their trust
under the shadow of thy wings.

Psalm 36:7 KJV

Because your love is better than life, my lips
will glorify you. I will praise you as long as I live,
and in your name I will lift up my hands.

Psalm 63:3-4 NIV

For you, O Lord, are good and forgiving,
abounding in steadfast love to all who call
upon you.

Psalm 86:5 ESV

But from everlasting to everlasting the
LORD's love is with those who fear him, and his
righteousness with their children's children.

Psalm 103:17 NIV

Jesus answered and said unto him, "If a man
love me, he will keep my words: and my
Father will love him, and we will come unto
him, and make our abode with him."

John 14:23 KJV

Whoever is wise will observe these things, and they will understand the lovingkindness of the LORD.

Psalm 107:43 NKJV

The LORD is gracious, and full of compassion; slow to anger, and of great mercy.

Psalm 145:8 KJV

Behold, what manner of love the Father hath bestowed upon us, that we should be called the sons of God: therefore the world knoweth us not, because it knew him not.

1 John 3:1 KJV

For I am convinced that neither death nor life, neither angels nor demons, neither the present nor the future, nor any powers, neither height nor depth, nor anything else in all creation, will be able to separate us from the love of God that is in Christ Jesus our Lord.

Romans 8:38-39 NIV

Indeed it was for my own peace that I had great bitterness; but You have lovingly delivered my soul from the pit of corruption; for You have cast all my sins behind Your back.

Isaiah 38:17 NKJV

The LORD opens the eyes of the blind. The
LORD lifts up those who are bowed down;
the LORD loves the righteous.

Psalm 146:8 ESV

The LORD appeared to us in the past, saying:
"I have loved you with an everlasting love;
I have drawn you with loving-kindness."

Jeremiah 31:3 NIV

"For God so loved the world that he gave
his only Son, that whoever believes in him
should not perish but have eternal life."

John 3:16 ESV

"For the Father himself loves you,
because you have loved Me, and have
believed that I came forth from God."

John 16:27 NKJV

God shows his love for us in that while we
were still sinners, Christ died for us.

Romans 5:8 ESV

But God, who is rich in mercy, because
of His great love with which He loved us,
even when we were dead in trespasses,
made us alive together with Christ.

Ephesians 2:4-5 NKJV

HELP

My God will meet all your needs according
to his glorious riches in Christ Jesus.

Philippians 4:19 NIV

How often have you sidestepped a task because you thought that you were unable to do it?

As long as you trust in your own abilities, there will be times when you shy away from a challenge or responsibility. The result is a feeling of failure or inadequacy and you could miss out on wonderful opportunities in life.

Remember that when God calls you to do something, He chooses you because He knows that you are the one to fulfill this specific calling. God does not necessarily call the ones who are able: He enables those whom He calls.

Whatever task you are called to do, pray about it and dedicate it to Christ. Seek the Holy Spirit's assistance and obediently and willingly follow wherever He leads you. You will not fail, because God Himself will be with you.

God's Ever-Present Help

God is our refuge and strength, an ever-present help in trouble.

Psalm 46:1 NIV

I will lift up mine eyes unto the hills, from whence cometh my help. My help cometh from the LORD, which made heaven and earth.

Psalm 121:1-2 KJV

The Spirit helps us in our weakness. For we do not know what to pray for as we ought, but the Spirit himself intercedes for us with groanings too deep for words.

Romans 8:26 ESV

God has said, "Never will I leave you; never will I forsake you." So we say with confidence, "The Lord is my helper; I will not be afraid. What can man do to me?"

Hebrews 13:5-6 NIV

In my distress I called to the LORD; I cried to my God for help. From his temple he heard my voice; my cry came before him, into his ears.

Psalm 18:6 NIV

Surely the arm of the LORD is not too short to save, nor his ear too dull to hear.

Isaiah 59:1 NIV

The LORD also will be a refuge for the oppressed, a refuge in times of trouble.

Psalm 9:9 NKJV

The LORD is good, a strong hold in the day of trouble; and he knoweth them that trust in him.

Nahum 1:7 KJV

For because he himself has suffered when tempted, he is able to help those who are being tempted.

Hebrews 2:18 ESV

He will deliver the needy when he cries, the poor also, and him who has no helper.

Psalm 72:12 NKJV

A righteous man may have many troubles, but the LORD delivers him from them all.

Psalm 34:19 NIV

I am poor and needy; make haste to me, O God! You are my help and my deliverer; O LORD, do not delay.

Psalm 70:5 NKJV

No harm will befall you, no disaster will come near your tent. For he will command his angels concerning you to guard you in all your ways.

Psalm 91:10-11 NIV

Our soul waiteth for the LORD:
he is our help and our shield.
Psalm 33:20 KJV

Surely God is my help; the Lord is the one who sustains me.

Psalm 54:4 NIV

Blessed is he whose help is in the God of Jacob,
whose hope is in the LORD his God.
Psalm 146:5 ESV

I love the LORD, because he hath heard my voice and my supplications. Because he hath inclined his ear unto me, therefore will I call upon him as long as I live.

Psalm 116:1-2 KJV

Help me, O LORD my God!
Oh, save me according to your mercy.
Psalm 109:26 NKJV

HOSPITALITY

"I was hungry and you gave me something to eat,
I was thirsty and you gave me something to drink."

Matthew 25:35 NIV

Hospitality is an instruction from God. "Offer hospitality to one another," Peter writes (1 Pet. 4:9 NIV). The Jews were very proud of their tradition of hospitality and it was built into several of their laws. In Genesis 18 you can read how hospitably Abraham received the three visitors. Such hospitality is disappearing from our modern society. When we hear that somebody wants to visit us, we first think about the time, effort and expense it will require.

True hospitality means to open your heart to visitors and make them feel truly welcome. Unfortunately the crime rate today makes it almost impossible for us to open our doors to strangers as in the past. This does not mean that we cannot try to live more hospitably toward our acquaintances; to care more for one other. We need to be genuinely compassionate and receive our friends in our homes with sincere hospitality.

Hospitality in Action

"Then the King will say to those on his right, 'Come, you who are blessed by my Father; take your inheritance, the kingdom prepared for you since the creation of the world. For I was hungry and you gave me something to eat, I was thirsty and you gave me something to drink, I was a stranger and you invited me in.'"

Matthew 25:34-35 NIV

"For truly, I say to you, whoever gives you a cup of water to drink because you belong to Christ will by no means lose his reward."

Mark 9:41 ESV

Share with God's people who are in need. Practice hospitality.

Romans 12:13 NIV

And they, continuing daily with one accord in the temple, and breaking bread from house to house, did eat their meat with gladness and singleness of heart.

Acts 2:46 KJV

If a brother or sister is poorly clothed and lacking in daily food, and one of you says to them, "Go in peace, be warmed and filled," without giving them the things needed for the body, what good is that?

James 2:15-16 ESV

Be hospitable to one another without grumbling. As each one has received a gift, minister it to one another, as good stewards of the manifold grace of God.

1 Peter 4:9-10 NKJV

Dear friend, you are faithful in what you are doing for the brothers, even though they are strangers to you. They have told the church about your love. You will do well to send them on their way in a manner worthy of God. It was for the sake of the Name that they went out, receiving no help from the pagans. We ought therefore to show hospitality to such men so that we may work together for the truth.

3 John 5-8 NIV

Do not neglect to show hospitality to strangers, for thereby some have entertained angels unawares.

Hebrews 13:2 ESV

As we have therefore opportunity, let us do good unto all men, especially unto them who are of the household of faith.

Galatians 6:10 KJV

Do not let a widow under sixty years old be taken into the number, and not unless she has been the wife of one man, well reported for good works: if she has brought up children, if she has lodged strangers, if she has washed the saints' feet, if she has relieved the afflicted, if she has diligently followed every good work.

1 Timothy 5:9-10 NKJV

"When you give a banquet, invite the poor, the crippled, the lame, the blind, and you will be blessed. Although they cannot repay you, you will be repaid at the resurrection of the righteous."

Luke 14:13 NIV

"I tell you the truth, whatever you did for one of the least of these brothers of mine, you did for me."

Matthew 25:40 NIV

This is the day
the LORD has made;
let us rejoice
and be glad in it.

~ Psalm 118:24, NIV

HOPE

Let your steadfast love, O Lord,
be upon us, even as we hope in you.

Psalm 33:22 ESV

Hope, a striking painting by Frederick Watts, hangs in the Tate Gallery in London. A beautiful, blindfolded woman is sitting on top of a globe. In her hand she holds a lute. All but one of the strings are broken. She touches the one string with her finger and bends forward, listening. She is filled with hope – believing the best in the worst possible circumstances.

As long as hope is alive, life cannot get us down; we will not snap under the weight of our problems and afflictions. God is able to turn the worst situations around.

Where hope exists, no night can be completely dark. Hope fills our hearts with joy even when our hearts are breaking.

It is hope that gives us an invincible spirit. This sinful world only knows about a hopeless end; the Christian knows an endless hope!

Hope that
will not Disappoint

Why art thou cast down, O my soul? and why art thou disquieted in me? Hope thou in God: for I shall yet praise him for the help of his countenance.

Psalm 42:5-6 KJV

In hope he believed against hope, that he should become the father of many nations, as he had been told, "So shall your offspring be."

Romans 4:18 ESV

We rejoice in the hope of the glory of God. Not only so, but we also rejoice in our sufferings, because we know that suffering produces perseverance; perseverance, character; and character, hope. And hope does not disappoint us, because God has poured out his love into our hearts by the Holy Spirit, whom he has given us.

Romans 5:2-5 NIV

Surely there is a future, and your hope will not be cut off.

Proverbs 23:18 ESV

May the God of hope fill you with all joy and peace in believing, so that by the power of the Holy Spirit you may abound in hope.

Romans 15:13 ESV

God has chosen to make known among the Gentiles the glorious riches of this mystery, which is Christ in you, the hope of glory.

Colossians 1:27 NIV

This hope we have as an anchor of the soul, both sure and steadfast, and which enters the Presence behind the veil.

Hebrews 6:19 NKJV

Therefore, prepare your minds for action; be self-controlled; set your hope fully on the grace to be given you when Jesus Christ is revealed.

1 Peter 1:13 NIV

For we were saved in this hope, but hope that is seen is not hope; for why does one still hope for what he sees? But if we hope for what we do not see, we eagerly wait for it with perseverance.

Romans 8:24-25 NKJV

Hope deferred maketh the heart sick: but
when the desire cometh, it is a tree of life.

Proverbs 13:12 KJV

The eyes of the LORD are on those
who fear him, on those whose
hope is in his unfailing love.

Psalm 33:18 NIV

O Israel, hope in the LORD; for with the LORD
there is mercy, and with Him is abundant
redemption.

Psalm 130:7-8 NKJV

You will feel secure, because there
is hope; you will look
around and take your rest in security.

Job 11:18 ESV

No one whose hope is in you will ever be
put to shame, but they will be put to shame
who are treacherous without excuse.

Psalm 25:3 NIV

Lead me in thy truth, and teach me:
for thou art the God of my
salvation; on thee do I wait all the day.

Psalm 25:5 KJV

JOY

Consider it pure joy, my brothers,
whenever you face trials of many kinds.

James 1:2 NIV

In Galatians 5:22-23 Paul speaks of the fruit of the Spirit. Firstly we find love. Secondly Paul mentions joy, an equally indispensable sign of salvation.

However, many people experience Christianity as somber and gloomy. This is a sad denial of the life of joy that should characterize the life of every Christian.

What the prodigal son missed most in the joyless country of sin, was the joyful feasting in his father's house. God's redeemed children on earth are invited to enjoy God's feast here and now. We accept His forgiveness but don't experience His joy in our daily lives. We longingly stand on the outskirts of joy, robbing ourselves of one of God's greatest gifts of grace.

Christian joy is the result of an encounter with the living Savior. In Christ God drew very near to us – in fact, He filled us. Our joy should be constant and eternal, because Christ is our Source.

Jubilant Joy

You have loved righteousness and hated wickedness; therefore God, your God, has set you above your companions by anointing you with the oil of joy.

Hebrews 1:9 NIV

This is the day the LORD has made;
let us rejoice and be glad in it.

Psalm 118:24 NIV

You make known to me the path of life; in your presence there is fullness of joy; at your right hand are pleasures forevermore.

Psalm 16:11 ESV

Those who sow in tears shall reap in joy. He who continually goes forth weeping, bearing seed for sowing, shall doubtless come again with rejoicing, bringing his sheaves with him.

Psalm 126:5-6 NKJV

For ye shall go out with joy, and be led forth with peace: the mountains and the hills shall break forth before you into singing, and all the trees of the field shall clap their hands.

Isaiah 55:12 KJV

The ransomed of the LORD shall return and come to Zion with singing; everlasting joy shall be upon their heads; they shall obtain gladness and joy, and sorrow and sighing shall flee away.

Isaiah 35:10 ESV

Though you have not seen him, you love him. Though you do not now see him, you believe in him and rejoice with joy that is inexpressible and filled with glory.

1 Peter 1:8 ESV

"Ask and you will receive, and your joy will be complete."

John 16:24 NIV

Rejoice in the Lord always. Again I will say, rejoice!

Philippians 4:4 NKJV

For this day is holy unto our LORD: neither be ye sorry; for the joy of the LORD is your strength.

Nehemiah 8:10 KJV

Let the righteous rejoice in the LORD and take refuge in him; let all the upright in heart praise him!

Psalm 64:10 NIV

You have put more joy in my heart than they
have when their grain and wine abound.

Psalm 4:7 ESV

I will greatly rejoice in the LORD, my soul
shall be joyful in my God; for he hath
clothed me with the garments of salvation.

Isaiah 61:10 KJV

The righteous shall be glad; they shall
exult before God; they shall be jubilant
with joy.

Psalm 68:3 ESV

Blessed are the people who know the
joyful sound! They walk, O LORD, in
the light of Your countenance. In Your
name they rejoice all day long, and in
Your righteousness they are exalted.

Psalm 89:15-16 NKJV

These things have I spoken unto you, that
my joy might remain in you, and that your
joy might be full.

John 15:11 KJV

KINDNESS

A kind man benefits himself,
but a cruel man brings trouble on himself.

Proverbs 11:17 NIV

Kindness, as it is used in the Bible, means to be kind-hearted. It is the good-naturedness of love. There are many Christians who are good people, but who tend to be unkind and constantly critical of everything.

The kindness of love strives for fairness toward God and your fellowman. In essence, faith requires loyalty and reliability and both are born from the love of God.

Kindness seeks only the best for your fellowmen, regardless of what they may do. It discards all bitterness and thoughts of revenge and lives in peace with everyone.

Love that is kind must be the distinctive characteristic of Christ's followers. Only then will we succeed in being His witnesses. Our kindness must be evident to all people; they will then ask about the source of our kindness and so find Jesus.

Kindness Accomplishes Much

He did good by giving you rains from heaven and fruitful seasons, satisfying your hearts with food and gladness.

Acts 14:17 ESV

"Then the King will say to those on his right,
'Come, you who are blessed by my Father;
take your inheritance, the kingdom prepared
for you since the creation of the world.
For I was hungry and you gave me
something to eat, I was thirsty and you gave
me something to drink, I was a stranger
and you invited me in, I needed clothes and
you clothed me, I was sick and you looked after
me, I was in prison and you came to visit me.'"

Matthew 25:34-36 NIV

Do you show contempt for the riches of his kindness, tolerance and patience, not realizing that God's kindness leads you toward repentance?

Romans 2:4 NIV

Finally, all of you be of one mind, having
compassion for one another; love as
brothers, be tenderhearted, be courteous.

1 Peter 3:8 NKJV

If you spend yourselves in behalf of the hungry and satisfy the needs of the oppressed, then your light will rise in the darkness, and your night will become like the noonday.

Isaiah 58:10 NIV

Be ye kind one to another, tenderhearted,
forgiving one another, even as
God for Christ's sake hath forgiven you.
Ephesians 4:32 KJV

Blessed are the merciful, for they shall obtain mercy.

Matthew 5:7 NKJV

You have granted me life and favor,
and Your care has preserved my spirit.
Job 10:12 NKJV

Do to others as you would have them do to you.

Luke 6:31 NIV

Blessed is he who is generous to the poor.
Proverbs 14:21 ESV

An anxious heart weighs a man down, but a kind word cheers him up.

Proverbs 12:25 NIV

The Lord's servant must not be quarrelsome but kind to everyone, patiently enduring evil.

2 Timothy 2:24 ESV

He who is kind to the poor lends to the LORD, and he will reward him for what he has done.

Proverbs 19:17 NIV

Giving all diligence, add to your faith virtue; and to virtue knowledge; and to knowledge temperance; and to temperance patience; and to patience godliness; and to godliness brotherly kindness; and to brotherly kindness charity.

2 Peter 1:5-7 KJV

Put on then, as God's chosen ones, holy and beloved, compassion, kindness, humility, meekness and patience.

Colossians 3:12 ESV

We have different gifts, according to the grace given us. If it is serving, let him serve; if it is teaching, let him teach; if it is encouraging, let him encourage; if it is contributing to the needs of others, let him give generously; if it is showing mercy, let him do it cheerfully.

Romans 12:6-8 NIV

Mercy and Compassion

The Lord is compassionate and merciful.
James 5:11 ESV

It is so easy to become overwhelmed by the suffering of others. There seems to be so much need and we wonder how our small contribution can help.

Instead of shrugging our shoulders and thinking it is of no use to try to help, we should allow the Holy Spirit to work through us. He is our eternal source of mercy and compassion.

Let Him lead and use us where we are most needed. We will no longer be overwhelmed by the plight of the needy, but empowered to alleviate distress exactly where God needs us to.

Allow yourself to become a channel of His mercy and compassion. He will empower you to make a difference in the lives of those around you.

Merciful Compassion

He passed in front of Moses, proclaiming, "The Lord, the Lord, the compassionate and gracious God, slow to anger, abounding in love and faithfulness, maintaining love to thousands, and forgiving wickedness, rebellion and sin. Yet he does not leave the guilty unpunished; he punishes the children and their children for the sin of the fathers to the third and fourth generation."

Exodus 34:6-7 NIV

All the paths of the Lord are steadfast love and faithfulness, for those who keep his covenant and his testimonies.

Psalm 25:10 ESV

Have mercy upon me, O God, according to thy lovingkindness: according unto the multitude of thy tender mercies blot out my transgressions.

Psalm 51:1 KJV

"But the tax collector stood at a distance. He would not even look up to heaven, but beat his breast and said, 'God, have mercy on me, a sinner.'"

Luke 18:13 NIV

I will not take my love from him, nor will I ever betray my faithfulness.

Psalm 89:33 NIV

You are a God ready to forgive,
gracious and merciful, slow to anger
and abounding in steadfast love.

Nehemiah 9:17 ESV

His mercy is for those who fear him from generation to generation.

Luke 1:50 ESV

It is of the LORD's mercies that we
are not consumed, because his
compassions fail not. They are new every
morning: great is thy faithfulness.

Lamentations 3:22-23 KJV

Be merciful, just as your Father also is merciful.

Luke 6:36 NKJV

Because of his great love for us, God, who is
rich in mercy, made us alive with Christ even
when we were dead in transgressions – it is
by grace you have been saved. And God
raised us up with Christ and seated us with
him in the heavenly realms in Christ Jesus.

Ephesians 2:4-6 NIV

A man who is kind benefits himself, but a cruel man hurts himself.

Proverbs 11:17 ESV

Let the wicked forsake his way,
and the unrighteous man his thoughts;
let him return to the LORD, and He
will have mercy on him, and to our God,
for He will abundantly pardon.

Isaiah 55:7 NKJV

Do not repay evil with evil or insult with insult, but with blessing, because to this you were called so that you may inherit a blessing.

1 Peter 3:9 NIV

Who is a God like You, pardoning iniquity
and passing over the transgression
of the remnant of His heritage? He does
not retain His anger forever, because
He delights in mercy. He will again have
compassion on us, and will subdue our
iniquities. You will cast all our sins into the
depths of the sea. You will give truth to Jacob
and mercy to Abraham, which You
have sworn to our fathers from days of old.

Micah 7:18-20 NKJV

PEACE

The LORD will give strength unto his people;
the LORD will bless his people with peace.

Psalm 29:11 KJV

There are times when you are bombarded with dreadful experiences. Very quickly you become stressed and your heart is filled with turmoil. You become tense and discouraged and your health begins to suffer.

We live in a stressful world, therefore it is imperative to develop inner reserves to draw strength from when things go wrong. The most important source of strength is the peace that Jesus Christ offers to those who love Him.

When things start going wrong and stress mounts, refuse to let it overwhelm you. Guard against becoming irritable. Control your thoughts and deliberately choose to remain calm. If it is at all possible, draw aside with Christ even if only for a few minutes. Reaffirm your dependence on Him. Remind yourself that His peace is available to you.

Very soon your spirit will become calm and His peace will refresh your heart.

BLESSINGS OF PEACE

Do not be anxious about anything, but in everything, by prayer and petition, with thanksgiving, present your requests to God. And the peace of God, which transcends all understanding, will guard your hearts and your minds in Christ Jesus.

Philippians 4:6-7 NIV

"Blessed are the peacemakers,
for they shall be called sons of God."
Matthew 5:9 NKJV

You will keep in perfect peace him whose mind is steadfast, because he trusts in you.

Isaiah 26:3 NIV

"Peace I leave with you, my peace
I give unto you: not as the world giveth,
give I unto you. Let not your heart
be troubled, neither let it be afraid."
John 14:27 KJV

The mind of sinful man is death, but the mind controlled by the Spirit is life and peace.

Romans 8:6 NIV

Great peace have those who love your law;
nothing can make them stumble.

Psalm 119:165 ESV

Consider the blameless, observe the upright;
there is a future for the man of peace.

Psalm 37:37 NIV

Then, the same day at evening, being the
first day of the week, when the doors were
shut where the disciples were assembled,
for fear of the Jews, Jesus came and stood
in the midst, and said to them, "Peace be
with you."

John 20:19 NKJV

In peace I will both lie down and sleep; for
you alone, O LORD, make me dwell in safety.

Psalm 4:8 ESV

Deceit is in the heart of those who devise
evil, but counselors of peace have joy.

Proverbs 12:20 NKJV

"I have said these things to you,
that in me you may have peace. In
the world you will have tribulation. But
take heart; I have overcome the world."

John 16:33 ESV

I will hear what God the LORD will speak:
for he will speak peace unto his people,
and to his saints.

Psalm 85:8 KJV

When a man's ways please the LORD, he makes
even his enemies to be at peace with him.

Proverbs 16:7 ESV

Therefore, since we have been justified
through faith, we have peace with God
through our Lord Jesus Christ.

Romans 5:1 NIV

"Glory to God in the highest, and on earth
peace to men on whom his favor rests."

Luke 2:14 NIV

Let the peace of Christ rule in your hearts,
since as members of one body you were
called to peace. And be thankful.

Colossians 3:15 NIV

Now the Lord of peace himself
give you peace always by all means.
The Lord be with you all.

2 Thessalonians 3:16 KJV

Every good and perfect gift is from above, coming down from the Father of the heavenly lights, who does not change like shifting shadows.

~ James 1:17, NIV

PERFECTION

By one sacrifice he has made perfect
forever those who are being made holy.

Hebrews 10:14 NIV

There is much emphasis on perfection in the world today. Some people are so obsessed with the perfection of material things that social and spiritual standards are neglected. The beauty of God's creation is marred by wasteful lifestyles and personal moral standards are ignored because of greed. Yet we are called to spiritual perfection.

There is only one worthwhile standard of perfection and that is the life that Christ gives His followers. Nothing else can ever give you true fulfillment because life in Christ is eternal and constant. There is no substitute for the Christian life.

Let God guide you as you sincerely pursue perfection and holiness. Dedicate everything that you do to Him; stay within His holy will in all you do and maintain the standards set by Jesus. Then you will achieve a degree of perfection far beyond anything you can imagine.

STRIVING FOR PERFECTION

He is the Rock, His work is perfect; for all His ways are justice, a God of truth and without injustice; righteous and upright is He.

Deuteronomy 32:4 NKJV

As for God, his way is perfect; the word of the LORD is flawless. He is a shield for all who take refuge in him. For who is God besides the LORD? And who is the Rock except our God? It is God who arms me with strength and makes my way perfect.

2 Samuel 22:31-33 NIV

The law of the LORD is perfect, converting the soul: the testimony of the LORD is sure, making wise the simple.

Psalm 19:7 KJV

Out of Zion, the perfection of beauty, God shines forth.

Psalm 50:2 ESV

We preach, warning every man, and teaching every man in all wisdom; that we may present every man perfect in Christ Jesus.

Colossians 1:28 KJV

O LORD, You are my God. I will exalt You,
I will praise Your name, for You have done
wonderful things.

Isaiah 25:1 NKJV

"Be ye therefore perfect, even as
your Father which is in heaven is perfect."
Matthew 5:48 KJV

Finally, brothers, rejoice. Aim for restora-
tion, comfort one another, agree with one
another, live in peace; and the God of love
and peace will be with you.

2 Corinthians 13:11 ESV

Not that I have already obtained
all this, or have already been made perfect,
but I press on to take hold of that
for which Christ Jesus took hold of me.
Philippians 3:12 NIV

By one sacrifice he has made perfect forever
those who are being made holy.

Hebrews 10:14 NIV

Every good and perfect gift is
from above, coming down from the
Father of the heavenly lights, who
does not change like shifting shadows.
James 1:17 NIV

Let us fix our eyes on Jesus, the author and perfecter of our faith.

Hebrews 12:2 NIV

It was he who gave some to be apostles,
some to be prophets, some to be evangelists,
and some to be pastors and teachers,
to prepare God's people for works of service,
so that the body of Christ may be built up
until we all reach unity in the faith and in
the knowledge of the Son of God and
become mature, attaining to the whole
measure of the fullness of Christ.

Ephesians 4:11-13 NIV

You have come to the assembly of the firstborn who are enrolled in heaven, and to God, the judge of all, and to the spirits of the righteous made perfect.

Hebrews 12:22-23 ESV

Do not be conformed to this world,
but be transformed by the renewing of your
mind, that you may prove what is that good
and acceptable and perfect will of God.

Romans 12:2 NKJV

That the man of God may be perfect, thoroughly furnished unto all good works.

2 Timothy 3:17 KJV

The Presence of God

You hem me in, behind and before;
and lay your hand upon me.
Psalm 139:5 ESV

People seldom experience the presence of God in exactly the same way. One of the great mysteries of the Christian faith is that God reveals Himself to His children according to their personal circumstances and needs.

Many Christians are discouraged when they hear of the experiences of others who have felt the touch of Jesus in their lives, and who have experienced unforgettable moments of joy in which they knew without a doubt that they were in the presence of the risen Christ.

If you feel discouraged, remember that you are a very special person. Not only are you His unique creation, but you are His child and as your heavenly Father He knows your needs better than you know them yourself.

All you need to do is wait quietly for Him and know that He is God.

Dwelling in God's Presence

Keep your lives free from the love of money and be content with what you have, because God has said, "Never will I leave you; never will I forsake you."

Hebrews 13:5 NIV

"The virgin will be with child and will give birth to a son, and they will call him Immanuel" – which means, "God with us."

Matthew 1:23 NIV

"I will make my dwelling among you, and my soul shall not abhor you. And I will walk among you and will be your God, and you shall be my people."

Leviticus 26:11-12 ESV

"Whoever has my commands and keeps them, he it is who loves me. And he who loves me will be loved by my Father, and I will love him and manifest myself to him."

John 14:21 ESV

Jesus answered and said to him, "If anyone loves Me, he will keep My word; and My Father will love him, and We will come to him and make Our home with him."

John 14:23 NKJV

"For where two or three are gathered together in my name, there am I in the midst
of them."

Matthew 18:20 KJV

"Remain in me, and I will remain in you.
No branch can bear fruit by itself; it must
remain in the vine. Neither can you bear fruit
unless you remain in me. I am the vine; you
are the branches. If a man remains in me
and I in him, he will bear much fruit; apart
from me you can do nothing. If you remain
in me and my words remain in you, ask
whatever you wish, and it will be given you."

John 15:4-7 NIV

"And surely I am with you always, to the
very end of the age."

Matthew 28:20 NIV

As for me, I am poor and needy, but the
Lord takes thought for me. You are my help
and my deliverer; do not delay, O my God!

Psalm 40:17 ESV

The LORD is near to all who call on him, to
all who call on him in truth. He fulfills the
desires of those who fear him; he hears their
cry and saves them.

Psalm 145:18-19 NIV

He that keepeth his commandments dwelleth in him, and he in him. And hereby we know that he abideth in us, by the Spirit which he hath given us.

1 John 3:24 KJV

"Behold, I stand at the door and knock.
If anyone hears my voice and opens
the door, I will come in to him
and eat with him, and he with me."

Revelation 3:20 ESV

For thus says the One who is high and lifted up, who inhabits eternity, whose name is Holy: "I dwell in the high and holy place, and also with him who is of a contrite and lowly spirit, to revive the spirit of the lowly, and to revive the heart of the contrite."

Isaiah 57:15 ESV

Sing to God, sing praise to his name, extol him who rides on the clouds – his name is the LORD – and rejoice before him. A father to the fatherless, a defender of widows, is God in his holy dwelling. God sets the lonely in families, he leads forth the prisoners with singing; but the rebellious live in a sun-scorched land.

Psalm 68:4-6 NIV

PROTECTION

The LORD will keep you from all
harm – he will watch over your life.

Psalm 121:7 NIV

We can never drift out of the reach of God's love and omnipotence. He will never forsake us. His eyes continuously move over all the earth in order to help those who trust in Him. He shelters them in times of danger, helps them handle temptations and problems and comforts them in sorrow.

What a blessed privilege it is to have such a God as our protector. If we live within His will, wherever we find ourselves, we can rest assured that He keeps a loving watch over us and that He will hear when we call on Him.

It is a privilege to know that, wherever you may go, He constantly watches over you. If we walk in His path and do His will every moment of the day, we will have the assurance in our hearts that our Master and Savior is always near us to protect us and provide for us.

PROMISES OF PROTECTION

The LORD is my shepherd, I shall not be in want. He makes me lie down in green pastures, he leads me beside quiet waters, he restores my soul. He guides me in paths of righteousness for his name's sake. Even though I walk through the valley of the shadow of death, I will fear no evil, for you are with me; your rod and your staff, they comfort me. You prepare a table before me in the presence of my enemies. You anoint my head with oil; my cup overflows. Surely goodness and love will follow me all the days of my life, and I will dwell in the house of the LORD forever.

Psalm 23 NIV

Let all those that put their trust in thee
rejoice: let them ever shout for joy,
because thou defendest them: let them
also that love thy name be joyful in thee.

Psalm 5:11 KJV

The angel of the LORD encamps all around those who fear Him, and delivers them. Oh, taste and see that the LORD is good; blessed is the man who trusts in Him!

Psalm 34:7-8 NKJV

My God shall supply all your need according
to His riches in glory by Christ Jesus.

Philippians 4:19 NKJV

O LORD, you will keep us safe and
protect us from such people forever.

Psalm 12:7 NIV

"Because he holds fast to me in love, I will
deliver him; I will protect him, for he knows
my name. When he calls to me, I will answer
him; I will be with him in trouble; I will
rescue him and honor him."

Psalm 91:14-15 ESV

God is able to make all grace
abound to you, so that having all
sufficiency in all things at all times,
you may abound in every good work.

2 Corinthians 9:8 ESV

The LORD gives strength to his people; the
LORD blesses his people with peace.

Psalm 29:11 NIV

The LORD is my portion and
my cup; you hold my lot.

Psalm 16:5 ESV

Oh, fear the LORD, you His saints! There is no want to those who fear Him. The young lions lack and suffer hunger, but those who seek the LORD shall not lack any good thing.

Psalm 34:9-10 NKJV

"Fear thou not; for I am with thee: be not dismayed; for I am thy God: I will strengthen thee; yea, I will help thee; yea, I will uphold thee with the right hand of my righteousness."

Isaiah 41:10 KJV

The name of the LORD is a strong tower; the righteous run to it and are safe.

Proverbs 18:10 NIV

You are a hiding place for me;
you preserve me from trouble; you
surround me with shouts of deliverance.

Psalm 32:7 ESV

Surely he will save you from the fowler's snare and from the deadly pestilence. He will cover you with his feathers, and under his wings you will find refuge; his faithfulness will be your shield and rampart.

Psalm 91:3-4 NIV

PURITY

"Sanctify them by your truth, your word is truth."
John 17:17 NIV

Real goodness is very appealing. Sham goodness is repulsive. This was the essential difference between Christ and the Scribes and Pharisees. Wherever He went, the throngs followed Him because they saw in Him a purity they had never seen in any other person. They wanted to understand it better and obtain it for themselves.

The awfulness of sin and its terrible results can be stressed, the need for repentance can be expounded. Yet, it is only when people see the beauty of the risen Savior that they begin to understand something of His love for them. Only then are their hearts softened.

But how can holiness ever be understood and the light of Christ be noticed, other than in the lives of Christian disciples? This seems like an impossible challenge and yet, because Christ promised to dwell in those who believe in Him, it is a glorious possibility.

THE PATH TO PURITY

How much more will the blood of Christ, who through the eternal Spirit offered himself without blemish to God, purify our conscience from dead works to serve the living God.

Hebrews 9:14 ESV

If we walk in the light, as he is in the light,
we have fellowship with one another,
and the blood of Jesus, his Son, purifies
us from all sin. If we claim to be without sin,
we deceive ourselves and the truth is not in us.
If we confess our sins, he is faithful
and just and will forgive us our sins and
purify us from all unrighteousness.

1 John 1:7-9 NIV

The statutes of the LORD are right, rejoicing the heart; the commandment of the LORD is pure, enlightening the eyes.

Psalm 19:8 NKJV

Draw near to God and he will draw near
to you. Cleanse your hands, you sinners;
and purify your hearts, you double-minded.

James 4:8 NKJV

Our citizenship is in heaven, and from it we await a Savior, the Lord Jesus Christ, who will transform our lowly body to be like his glorious body, by the power that enables him even to subject all things to himself.

Philippians 3:20-21 ESV

Do everything without complaining
or arguing, so that you may become blameless
and pure, children of God without fault
in a crooked and depraved generation,
in which you shine like stars in the universe

Philippians 2:14-15 NIV

Everyone who has this hope in Him purifies himself, just as He is pure.

1 John 3:3 NKJV

If, because of one man's trespass, death
reigned through that one man, much more
will those who receive the abundance of
grace and the free gift of righteousness reign
in life through the one man Jesus Christ.

Romans 5:17 ESV

You were washed, you were sanctified, you were justified in the name of the Lord Jesus Christ and by the Spirit of our God.

1 Corinthians 6:11 ESV

Your eyes are too pure to look on evil; you cannot tolerate wrong.

Habakkuk 1:13 NIV

The Lord knoweth how to deliver the godly out of temptations, and to reserve the unjust unto the day of judgment to be punished.

2 Peter 2:9 KJV

Do not share in the sins of others. Keep yourself pure.

1 Timothy 5:22 NIV

It is God's will that you should be sanctified: that you should avoid sexual immorality; that each of you should learn to control his own body in a way that is holy and honorable, not in passionate lust like the heathen, who do not know God; and that in this matter no one should wrong his brother or take advantage of him. The Lord will punish men for all such sins, as we have already told you and warned you.

1 Thessalonians 4:3-6 NIV

Just as He chose us in Him before the foundation of the world, that we should be holy and without blame before Him in love.

Ephesians 1:4 NKJV

Purpose and Potential

He who has prepared us for this very thing is God,
who has given us the Spirit as a guarantee.

2 Corinthians 5:5 ESV

For many people life is nothing but a monotonous routine. Day in and day out they go through the motions and constantly wonder if life has any meaning. Others are ambitious and want to reach the top in their profession, but often sacrifice integrity in order to obtain riches and prestige.

But there comes a time when every person starts seeking the real meaning of life. The only satisfying answer is a spiritual one. People who have a sincere and vibrant relationship with the living Christ have found the answer to this question. They live a purposeful life through the power of Christ.

The glorious truth is that people were created to glorify, worship and serve God. When God is at the center of a life, He pours out His blessing and life begins to reveal its deep secrets. When your purpose in life is to serve God and your fellowmen, you discover the deeper meaning of life.

Lasting Purpose
and True Potential

Now to each one the manifestation of the Spirit is given for the common good. To one there is given through the Spirit the message of wisdom, to another the message of knowledge by means of the same Spirit, to another faith by the same Spirit, to another gifts of healing by that one Spirit, to another miraculous powers, to another prophecy, to another distinguishing between spirits, to another speaking in different kinds of tongues, and to still another the interpretation of tongues. All these are the work of one and the same Spirit, and he gives them to each one, just as he determines.

1 Corinthians 12:7-11 NIV

I can do all things through
him who strengthens me.
Philippians 4:13 ESV

I am sure of this, that he who began a good work in you will bring it to completion at the day of Jesus Christ.

Philippians 1:6 ESV

Therefore, my beloved, as you have always obeyed, not as in my presence only, but now much more in my absence, work out your own salvation with fear and trembling; for it is God who works in you both to will and to do for His good pleasure.

Philippians 2:12-13 NKJV

That He might make known the
riches of his glory on the vessels of mercy,
which he had afore prepared unto glory,
even us, whom he hath called, not of
the Jews only, but also of the Gentiles?

Romans 9:23-24 KJV

We know that all things work together for good to those who love God, to those who are the called according to His purpose.

Romans 8:28 NKJV

Trust in the LORD with all thine heart;
and lean not unto thine own understanding.
In all thy ways acknowledge him,
and he shall direct thy paths.

Proverbs 3:5-6 KJV

Teach me to do Your will, for You are my God; Your Spirit is good. Lead me in the land of uprightness.

Psalm 143:10 NKJV

You are my lamp, O LORD; the LORD turns my darkness into light. With your help I can advance against a troop; with my God I can scale a wall.

2 Samuel 22:29-30 NIV

He made known to us the mystery of his will according to his good pleasure, which he purposed in Christ, to be put into effect when the times will have reached their fulfillment – to bring all things in heaven and on earth together under one head, even Christ.

Ephesians 1:9-10 NIV

"For this purpose I have raised you up, to show you my power, so that my name may be proclaimed in all the earth."

Exodus 9:16 ESV

The counsel of the LORD stands forever, the plans of His heart to all generations.

Psalm 33:11 NKJV

I will cry unto God most high; unto God that performeth all things for me.

Psalm 57:2 KJV

For surely, O LORD,
you bless the righteous;
you surround them
with your favor as with a shield.

~ Psalm 5:12, NIV

REWARD

The Lord bestows favor and honor;
no good thing does he withhold
from those whose walk is blameless.

Psalm 84:11 NIV

Many disillusioned people believe it is not worthwhile to do good. They have many arguments to justify their viewpoint. Sadly they concentrate only on the earthly here and now.

Remember, life does not begin and end with what we experience on earth alone. Whatever happens in our lives, whether trials or joys, our conduct and attitudes towards others prepare us for the eternal life that lies ahead.

God is the ultimate almighty Judge. Always try to honor Him. You may be suffering now but God will reward you for the way you lived on earth. Concentrate on radiating Jesus in your life every day. Ask God to enable you to hold on to the guidelines and standards that He has set for you so that your life will be pleasing to Him.

Reward for the Faithful

After these things the word of the Lord came to Abram in a vision: "Fear not, Abram, I am your shield; your reward shall be very great."

Genesis 15:1 ESV

I have fought a good fight, I have finished my course, I have kept the faith: Henceforth there is laid up for me a crown of righteousness, which the Lord, the righteous judge, shall give me at that day: and not to me only, but unto all them also that love his appearing.

2 Timothy 4:7-8 KJV

"Behold, I am coming soon, bringing my recompense with me, to repay everyone for what he has done."

Revelation 22:12 ESV

Praise be to the God and Father of our Lord Jesus Christ! In his great mercy he has given us new birth into a living hope through the resurrection of Jesus Christ from the dead, and into an inheritance that can never perish, spoil or fade – kept in heaven for you.

1 Peter 1:3-4 NIV

Without faith it is impossible to please him: for he that cometh to God must believe that he is, and that he is a rewarder of them that diligently seek him.

Hebrews 11:6 KJV

"Rejoice and be glad, for your reward is great in heaven, for so they persecuted the prophets who were before you."
Matthew 5:12 ESV

The nations were angry, and Your wrath has come, and the time of the dead, that they should be judged, and that You should reward Your servants the prophets and the saints, and those who fear Your name, small and great, and should destroy those who destroy the earth.

Revelation 11:18 NKJV

"Behold, the devil shall cast some of you into prison, that ye may be tried; and ye shall have tribulation ten days: be thou faithful unto death, and I will give thee a crown of life."
Revelation 2:10 KJV

When Christ who is your life appears, then you also will appear with Him in glory.
Colossians 3:4 NKJV

Blessed is the man who remains steadfast under trial, for when he has stood the test he will receive the crown of life, which God has promised to those who love him.

James 1:12 ESV

When the Chief Shepherd appears,
you will receive the crown
of glory that will never fade away.

1 Peter 5:4 NIV

Now he who plants and he who waters are one, and each will receive his own reward according to his own labor.

1 Corinthians 3:8 NKJV

Mankind will say, "Surely there
is a reward for the righteous; surely
there is a God who judges on earth."

Psalm 58:11 ESV

"Him who overcomes I will make a pillar in the temple of my God. Never again will he leave it. I will write on him the name of my God and the name of the city of my God, the new Jerusalem, which is coming down out of heaven from my God; and I will also write on him my new name."

Revelation 3:12 NIV

RICHES

You will be made rich in every way so that
you can be generous on every occasion.
2 Corinthians 9:11 NIV

Wealth can be a blessing or a curse, depending on the priority it takes in your life. It is tragic when the pursuit of wealth becomes a driving force.

When money becomes an idol it is so demanding that it destroys everything beautiful and worthwhile in one's character. The wealthy often look down on those who have nothing, and such people then become hard-hearted.

If money is kept in the right place on our priority list, it can be a great blessing. It cannot buy those qualities that are essential for true life. It might make your life more comfortable, but there are assets that are free, yet essential for true life.

We need a constant reminder that money can buy a bed, but not peaceful sleep; food, but not appetite; entertainment, but not happiness; luxuries, but not culture; a Bible, but not heaven. People often forget that the most valuable things in life are free.

Riches Beyond Measure

"He that is faithful in that which is least is faithful also in much: and he that is unjust in the least is unjust also in much. If therefore ye have not been faithful in the unrighteous mammon, who will commit to your trust the true riches?"

Luke 16:10-11 KJV

"Do not store up for yourselves treasures on earth, where moth and rust destroy, and where thieves break in and steal. But store up for yourselves treasures in heaven, where moth and rust do not destroy, and where thieves do not break in and steal."

Matthew 6:19-20 NIV

You may say to yourself, "My power and the strength of my hands have produced this wealth for me." But remember the LORD your God, for it is he who gives you the ability to produce wealth, and so confirms his covenant, which he swore to your forefathers, as it is today.

Deuteronomy 8:17-18 NIV

This grace was given, to preach to the Gentiles the unsearchable riches of Christ.

Ephesians 3:8 ESV

Better is a little with the fear of the LORD, than great treasure with trouble. Better is a dinner of herbs where love is, than a fatted calf with hatred.

Proverbs 15:16-17 NKJV

The days of the blameless are known to the LORD, and their inheritance will endure forever. In times of disaster they will not wither; in days of famine they will enjoy plenty.

Psalm 37:18-19 NIV

I have been young, and now am old; yet have I not seen the righteous forsaken, nor his seed begging bread. He is ever merciful, and lendeth; and his seed is blessed.

Psalm 37:25-26 KJV

Do not wear yourself out to get rich; have the wisdom to show restraint. Cast but a glance at riches, and they are gone, for they will surely sprout wings and fly off to the sky like an eagle.

Proverbs 23:4-5 NIV

Honor the LORD with your wealth and with the firstfruits of all your produce; then your barns will be filled with plenty, and your vats will be bursting with wine.

Proverbs 3:9-10 ESV

Godliness with contentment is great gain.
For we brought nothing into this world, and
it is certain we can carry nothing out.

1 Timothy 6:6-7 KJV

Command those who are rich in this
present age not to be haughty, nor to trust
in uncertain riches but in the living God,
who gives us richly all things to enjoy.

1 Timothy 6:17 NKJV

Riches do no profit in the day of wrath, but
righteousness delivers from death.

Proverbs 11:4 NKJV

Keep your life free from love of money, and
be content with what you have, for he has said,
"I will never leave you nor forsake you."

Hebrews 13:5 ESV

A little that the righteous man has is better
than the riches of many wicked. For the
arms of the wicked shall be broken, but the
LORD upholds the righteous.

Psalm 37:16-17 NKJV

Whoever trusts in his riches will fall, but the
righteous will flourish like a green leaf.

Proverbs 11:28 ESV

Righteousness

*"Blessed are those who hunger and thirst
for righteousness, for they shall be satisfied."*

Matthew 5:6 ESV

The Bible tells us clearly that we are all sinners and that we all fall short of the glory of God. But if you ask God to forgive your sins, it is futile to constantly remind yourself of them. If God has forgiven you, you must forgive yourself.

When God forgave your sins, He made you new, "Therefore, if anyone is in Christ, he is a new creation; the old has gone, the new has come. All this is from God" (2 Cor. 5:17-18 NIV).

God made you new and the righteousness that He gave you should have a positive influence on your life. Allow God's goodness to take root and to grow in you.

When the Master saves you and gives you His Spirit, He also gives you a dynamic goodness that is a rich blessing to you and to all those around you.

Assured Righteousness

He believed the Lord, and He accounted
it to him for righteousness.

Genesis 15:6 NKJV

The work of righteousness shall be
peace; and the effect of righteousness
quietness and assurance for ever.

Isaiah 32:17 KJV

"Seek first the kingdom of God and His
righteousness, and all these things shall be
added to you."

Matthew 6:33 NKJV

This righteousness from God comes through
faith in Jesus Christ to all who believe.
There is no difference, for all have sinned
and fall short of the glory of God, and are
justified freely by his grace through the
redemption that came by Christ Jesus.

Romans 3:22-24 NIV

For Christ also hath once suffered for sins,
the just for the unjust, that he might bring
us to God, being put to death in the flesh,
but quickened by the Spirit.

1 Peter 3:18 KJV

For surely, O LORD, you bless the righteous;
you surround them with your favor as with
a shield.

Psalm 5:12 NIV

Many are the afflictions of the righteous,
but the LORD delivers him out of them all.

Psalm 34:19 NKJV

The path of the righteous is like the light of
dawn, which shines brighter and brighter
until full day.

Proverbs 4:18 ESV

It shall be our righteousness, if we observe
to do all these commandments before the
LORD our God, as he hath commanded us.

Deuteronomy 6:25 KJV

The righteous will shine forth as the sun in
the kingdom of their Father. He who has
ears to hear, let him hear!

Matthew 13:43 NKJV

Henceforth there is laid for me the
crown of righteousness, which the Lord,
the righteous judge, will award to me on
that Day, and not only to me but also
to all who have loved his appearing.

2 Timothy 4:8 ESV

For our sake he made him to be sin who knew no sin, so that in him we might become the righteousness of God.

2 Corinthians 5:21 ESV

What is more, I consider everything a loss compared to the surpassing greatness of knowing Christ Jesus my Lord, for whose sake I have lost all things. I consider them rubbish, that I may gain Christ and be found in him, not having a righteousness of my own that comes from the law, but that which is through faith in Christ – the righteousness that comes from God and is by faith.

Philippians 3:8-9 NIV

Now the fruit of righteousness is sown in peace by those who make peace.

James 3:18 NKJV

For the LORD knows the way of the righteous, but the way of the wicked will perish.

Psalm 1:6 ESV

For the LORD God is a sun and shield; the LORD bestows favor and honor; no good thing does he withhold from those whose walk is blameless.

Psalm 84:11 NIV

Sanctification

The very God of peace sanctify you wholly;
and I pray God your whole spirit and
soul and body be preserved blameless
unto the coming of our Lord Jesus Christ.
1 Thessalonians 5:23 KJV

To be holy requires intimate fellowship with God. Some people reject the very idea of holiness as impractical as it requires high moral standards as well as total commitment to God. A truly holy person obeys Him implicitly in every area of his life.

A sanctified lifestyle requires you to be in control of all your attitudes and actions. You cannot hold on to the world with one hand while stretching the other hand half-heartedly toward God.

The guidelines for leading a holy life are clearly set out in God's Word. Christ is our perfect Example. He sent His Holy Spirit to dwell in us and lead us into the truth of sanctification. The more sensitive we become to the voice of the Holy Spirit, the more progress we will make on the road to sanctification.

On the Path to Holiness

For just as you once presented your members as slaves to impurity and to lawlessness leading to more lawlessness, so now present your members as slaves to righteousness leading to sanctification.

Romans 6:19 ESV

Therefore, I urge you, brothers, in view of God's mercy, to offer your bodies as living sacrifices, holy and pleasing to God – this is your spiritual act of worship. Do not conform any longer to the pattern of this world, but be transformed by the renewing of your mind. Then you will be able to test and approve what God's will is – his good, pleasing and perfect will.

Romans 12:1-2 NIV

For this is the will of God, your sanctification: that you should abstain from sexual immorality; that each of you should know how to possess his own vessel in sanctification and honor.

1 Thessalonians 4:3-4 NKJV

In Him we have redemption through His blood, the forgiveness of sins, according to the riches of His grace which He made to abound toward us in all wisdom and prudence.

Ephesians 1:7-8 NKJV

God, who saved us and called us to a holy calling, not because of our works but because of his own purpose and grace, which he gave us in Christ Jesus before the ages began.

2 Timothy 1:8-9 ESV

For they that are after the flesh do mind the things of the flesh; but they that are after the Spirit the things of the Spirit.

Romans 8:5 KJV

In Him you were also circumcised with the circumcision made without hands, by putting off the body of the sins of the flesh, by the circumcision of Christ.

Colossians 2:11 NKJV

All Scripture is God-breathed and is useful for teaching, rebuking, correcting and training in righteousness, so that the man of God may be thoroughly equipped for every good work.

2 Timothy 3:16-17 NIV

God's elect who have been chosen according to the foreknowledge of God the Father, through the sanctifying work of the Spirit, for obedience to Jesus Christ and sprinkling by his blood.

1 Peter 1:1-2 NIV

Know that a man is not justified by observing the law, but by faith in Jesus Christ. So we, too, have put our faith in Christ Jesus that we may be justified by faith in Christ and not by observing the law, because by observing the law no one will be justified.

Galatians 2:16-17 NIV

You have upheld me because of my integrity, and set me in your presence forever.

Psalm 41:12 ESV

For your name's sake, O LORD, preserve my life; in your righteousness, bring me out of trouble. In your unfailing love, silence my enemies; destroy all my foes, for I am your servant.

Psalm 143:11-12 NIV

For he chose us in him before the creation of the world to be holy and blameless.

Ephesians 1:4 NIV

SATISFACTION

"With long life will I satisfy him,
and shew him my salvation."

Psalm 91:16 KJV

We all yearn for inner peace and calm as the uncertainty in the world creates a sense of agitation. Our troubles are endless, and the consequences are always the same: anxiety and stress.

At times like these we need to go to God in prayer. He is the only One who can satisfy our desire for peace and security in the midst of life's anxieties.

Have faith that is firmly anchored in Jesus Christ and remain consistently and consciously in Him. He will show you how to handle all pressure and tension.

It may be difficult for you to fully understand His peace, but you will recognize it when it flows through you, calming all your fears and satisfying all your needs. Experience the peace of God, which transcends all understanding, and be completely satisfied in Christ.

Promises that Satisfy

If they listen and serve him, they complete
their days in prosperity, and their years in
in pleasantness.

Job 36:11 ESV

The fear of the LORD leads to life,
and he who has it will abide in satisfaction;
he will not be visited with evil.

Proverbs 19:23 NKJV

I am not saying this because I am in need,
for I have learned to be content whatever
the circumstances. I know what it is to be in
need, and I know what it is to have plenty.
I have learned the secret of being content
in any and every situation, whether well
fed or hungry, whether living in plenty or
in want.

Philippians 4:11-12 NIV

Godliness with contentment is great gain.
For we brought nothing into this world,
and it is certain we can carry
nothing out. And having food and
raiment let us be therewith content.

1 Timothy 6:6-8 KJV

Keep your life free from love of money, and be content with what you have, for he has said, "I will never leave you nor forsake you."

Hebrews 13:5 ESV

When you have eaten and are satisfied, praise the LORD your God for the good land he has given you.

Deuteronomy 8:10 NIV

As for me, I will see Your face in righteousness; I shall be satisfied when I awake in Your likeness.

Psalm 17:15 NKJV

The afflicted shall eat and be satisfied; those who seek him shall praise the Lord! May your hearts live forever!

Psalm 22:26 ESV

My soul shall be satisfied as with marrow and fatness; and my mouth shall praise thee with joyful lips.

Psalm 63:5 KJV

"He would have fed them also with the finest of wheat; and with honey from the rock I would have satisfied you."

Psalm 81:16 NKJV

When the LORD your God brings you into the land he swore to your fathers, to Abraham, Isaac and Jacob, to give you – a land with large, flourishing cities you did not build, houses filled with all kinds of good things you did not provide, wells you did not dig, and vineyards and olive groves you did not plant – then when you eat and are satisfied, be careful that you do not forget the LORD, who brought you out of Egypt, out of the land of slavery.

Deuteronomy 6:10-12 NIV

Satisfy us in the morning with
your steadfast love, that we may
rejoice and be glad all our days.
Psalm 90:14 ESV

Praise the LORD, O my soul, and forget not all his benefits – who forgives all your sins and heals all your diseases, who redeems your life from the pit and crowns you with love and compassion, who satisfies your desires with good things so that your youth is renewed like the eagle's.

Psalm 103:2-5 NIV

You open your hand; you satisfy
the desire of every living thing.
Psalm 145:16 ESV

The LORD is near to all
who call upon Him, to all
who call upon Him in truth.

~ Psalm 145:18, NKJV

SERVICE

Whatever you do, do it heartily,
as to the Lord and not to men.

Colossians 3:23 NKJV

F ew things give as much satisfaction as a task done to the best of your ability for the honor of your heavenly Father. To undertake and to grapple with a task you believe is the will of God and to then experience the satisfaction of success, gives deep and lasting satisfaction.

This feeling of achievement lifts your spirit and brings about great joy. If you faithfully performed one task, God will probably have more that He will entrust to you. When you have proven your value once, you should humbly ask God where He wants to use you next.

A true servant lives very close to the source of godly inspiration and spiritual refreshment. The soul of man flourishes on a job well done and the knowledge that he has done his best for God. Then God blesses all his labor. May this encourage you in your service to the Master.

Satisfaction through Service

Now being made free from sin, and become servants to God, ye have your fruit unto holiness, and the end everlasting life.

Romans 6:22 KJV

As each one has received a gift,
minister it to one another, as good
stewards of the manifold grace of God.

1 Peter 4:10 NKJV

In everything that he undertook in the service of God's temple and in obedience to the law and the commands, he sought his God and worked wholeheartedly. And so he prospered.

2 Chronicles 31:21 NIV

Then Jesus said to him,
"Away with you, Satan! For it is written
'You shall worship the Lord your God,
and Him only you shall serve.'"

Matthew 4:10 NKJV

So then, as we have opportunity, let us do good to everyone, and especially to those who are of the household of faith.

Galatians 6:10 ESV

"But so shall it not be among you: but who-soever will be great among you, shall be your minister: and whosoever of you will be the chiefest, shall be servant of all. For even the Son of man came not to be ministered unto, but to minister, and to give his life a ransom for many."

Mark 10:43-45 KJV

Do not be slothful in zeal,
be fervent in spirit, serve the Lord.
Romans 12:11 ESV

Stay dressed for action and keep your lamps burning.

Luke 12:35 ESV

"Whoever gives one of these little
ones even a cup of cold water because
he is a disciple, truly, I say to you,
he will by no means lose his reward."
Matthew 10:42 ESV

If any man speak, let him speak as the oracles of God; if any man minister, let him do it as of the ability which God giveth: that God in all things may be glorified through Jesus Christ, to whom be praise and dominion for ever and ever. Amen.

1 Peter 4:11 KJV

When he had finished washing their feet, he put on his clothes and returned to his place. "Do you understand what I have done for you?" he asked them. "You call me 'Teacher' and 'Lord,' and rightly so, for that is what I am. Now that I, your Lord and Teacher, have washed your feet, you also should wash one another's feet."

John 13:12-14 NIV

Make it your ambition to lead a quiet life,
to mind your own business and to
work with your hands, just as we told you,
so that your daily life may win
the respect of outsiders and so that you
will not be dependent on anybody.

1 Thessalonians 4:11-12 NIV

Obey them not only to win their favor when their eye is on you, but like slaves of Christ, doing the will of God from your heart. Serve wholeheartedly, as if you were serving the Lord, not men.

Ephesians 6:6-7 NIV

Jesus said to him, "No one, having
put his hand to the plow, and looking
back, is fit for the kingdom of God."

Luke 9:62 NKJV

TRUSTING GOD

Blessed is that man who makes the LORD
his trust, and does not respect
the proud, nor such as turn aside to lies.

Psalm 40:4 NKJV

There are so many things that can happen to us: many unexpected disappointments and ordeals can cross our paths at any time. Often we cannot understand or see the sense or meaning in them.

The Lord's love for us is endlessly tender and constructive. He assures us, "Never will I leave you; never will I forsake you" (Heb. 13:5 NIV). He wants us to trust Him where we cannot see. It is not a reckless leap in the dark, but sincere trust and faith that says, "I know for certain that God's will is best for me." This kind of faith leaves the choice to God. Then His peace will flow through us and result in joy.

Our faithful prayer each day must simply be, "Your will be done!" We must trust Him until we meet Him face to face. Then we will understand how His perfect will functions: always for our own good and to our benefit, even though it may not appear so.

A Simple Trust

Trust in the LORD and do good; dwell in the land and enjoy safe pasture. Delight yourself in the LORD and he will give you the desires of your heart. Commit your way to the LORD; trust in him.

Psalm 37:3-5 NIV

God is our refuge and strength,
a very present help in trouble.
Therefore we will not fear though
the earth gives way, though the mountains
be moved into the heart of the sea.

Psalm 46:1-2 ESV

For the LORD God is a sun and shield: the LORD will give grace and glory: no good thing will he withhold from them that walk uprightly. O LORD of hosts, blessed is the man that trusteth in thee.

Psalm 84:11-12 KJV

Without faith it is impossible to please him,
for whoever would draw near to
God must believe that he exists and
that he rewards those who seek him.

Hebrews 11:6 ESV

"Why do you worry about clothes? See how the lilies of the field grow. They do not labor or spin. Yet I tell you that not even Solomon in all his splendor was dressed like one of these. If that is how God clothes the grass of the field, which is here today and tomorrow is thrown into the fire, will he not much more clothe you, O you of little faith? So do not worry, saying, 'What shall we eat?' or 'What shall we drink?' or 'What shall we wear?' For the pagans run after all these things, and your heavenly Father knows that you need them. But seek first his kingdom and his righteousness, and all these things will be given to you as well."

Matthew 6:28-33 NIV

"Do not let your hearts be troubled.
Trust in God; trust also in me."
John 14:1 NIV

The LORD is good, a stronghold in the day of trouble; and He knows those who trust in Him.

Nahum 1:7 NKJV

Blessed is the man who trusts in the LORD,
whose trust is the Lord.
Jeremiah 17:7 ESV

Many sorrows shall be to the wicked; but he who trusts in the Lord, mercy shall surround him.

Psalm 32:10 NKJV

"Have faith in God," Jesus answered.
"I tell you the truth, if anyone says to this mountain, 'Go, throw yourself into the sea,' and does not doubt in his heart but believes that what he says will happen, it will be done for him. Therefore I tell you, whatever you ask for in prayer, believe that you have received it, and it will be yours."

Mark 11:22-24 NIV

Thou wilt keep him in perfect peace, whose mind is stayed on thee: because he trusteth in thee.

Isaiah 26:3 KJV

For whatever is born of God overcomes the world. And this is the victory that has overcome the world – our faith.

1 John 5:4 NKJV

I am crucified with Christ: nevertheless I live; yet not I, but Christ liveth in me: and the life which I now live in the flesh I live by the faith of the Son of God, who loved me, and gave himself for me.

Galatians 2:20 KJV

TRUTH

*Jesus answered, "I am the way and
the truth and the life. No one comes
to the Father except through me."*

John 14:6 NIV

All who sincerely seek the truth should humbly regard the questions of life. They must be willing to make new discoveries and to delve deeper than the obvious.

No student has ever found the boundary of truth, because truth has its source and fullness in God. Although the truth has many facets, they all originate with the holy, omniscient Creator God. All truth will lead you to a clearer understanding of the eternal God.

Even though no person can understand all truth, it is still possible for us to know the God of truth. Jesus said, "If you hold to my teaching, you are really my disciples. Then you will know the truth, and the truth will set you free" (John 8:31-32 NIV). Through obedience to the Lord, it is possible to be free from destructive forces that blind you to the truth. To love and to serve Christ is the starting point on the path of truth.

God's Promises are True

The LORD is the true God; He is the living God and the everlasting King.

Jeremiah 10:10 NKJV

"Whoever does what is true comes to the light, so that it may be clearly seen that his deeds have been carried out in God."

John 3:21 ESV

Then said Jesus to those Jews which believed on him, "If ye continue in my word, then are ye my disciples indeed; and ye shall know the truth, and the truth shall make you free."

John 8:31-32 KJV

When he, the Spirit of truth, comes, he will guide you into all truth. He will not speak on his own; he will speak only what he hears, and he will tell you what is yet to come.

John 16:13 NIV

"Sanctify them by Your truth. Your word is truth."

John 17:17 NKJV

You will know God's household, which is the church of the living God, the pillar and foundation of the truth.

1 Timothy 3:15 NIV

The law of the LORD is perfect, converting the soul: the testimony of the LORD is sure, making wise the simple. The statutes of the LORD are right, rejoicing the heart: the commandment of the LORD is pure, enlightening the eyes. The fear of the LORD is clean, enduring for ever: the judgments of the LORD are true and righteous altogether.

Psalm 19:7-9 KJV

Do your best to present yourself to God as one approved, a worker who has no need to be ashamed, rightly handling the word of truth.

2 Timothy 2:15 ESV

The LORD is near to all who call upon Him, to all who call upon Him in truth.

Psalm 145:18 NKJV

O LORD, who shall sojourn in your tent? Who shall dwell on your holy hill? He who walks blamelessly and does what is right and speaks truth in his heart.

Psalm 15:1-2 ESV

Therefore, since through God's mercy we have this ministry, we do not lose heart. Rather, we have renounced secret and shameful ways; we do not use deception, nor do we distort the word of God. On the contrary, by setting forth the truth plainly we commend ourselves to every man's conscience in the sight of God.

2 Corinthians 4:1-2 NIV

The words of the LORD are pure words,
like silver tried in a furnace of
earth, purified seven times.

Psalm 12:6 NKJV

For the word of the LORD is right and true; he is faithful in all he does.

Psalm 33:4 NIV

Send out your light and your truth;
let them lead me; let them bring me
to your holy hill and to your dwelling.

Psalm 43:3 ESV

"And this is life eternal, that they might know thee the only true God, and Jesus Christ, whom thou hast sent."

John 17:3 KJV

Victory

*For everyone born of God overcomes
the world. This is the victory that has
overcome the world, even our faith.*

1 John 5:4 NIV

Circumstances often fill us with fear and
we wonder how we could possibly have
landed in such situations.

Traumatic experiences, dramatic changes
in our personal lives or even mundane
everyday problems might cause us to feel
lost and seriously threatened.

The only way we could possibly cope
with life is in partnership with God. He created each one of us. He sent His Son to die
so that we may have eternal life. Therefore
He will not allow you to be defeated. He
will deliver you from evil.

It is crucial for you to have an intimate
relationship with Him. Then His Holy Spirit
will work in and through you and you will
be able to live victoriously in His Name.

Victorious Living

"Fear not, for I am with you; be not dismayed, for I am your God. I will strengthen you, Yes, I will help you, I will uphold you with My righteous right hand."

Isaiah 41:10 NKJV

"I have said these things to you,
that in me you may have peace. In the
world you will have tribulation. But
take heart; I have overcome the world."

John 16:33 ESV

What shall we then say to these things? If God be for us, who can be against us? Nay, in all these things we are more than conquerors through him that loved us.

Romans 8:31, 37 KJV

Then Jesus said to him, "Be gone, Satan!
For it is written, 'You shall worship the
Lord your God and him only shall you serve.'"
Then the devil left him, and behold, angels
came and were ministering to him.

Matthew 4:10-11 ESV

The God of peace will soon crush Satan under your feet. The grace of our Lord Jesus be with you.

Romans 16:20 NIV

Thanks be to God, who gives us the victory through our Lord Jesus Christ.

1 Corinthians 15:57 ESV

For the weapons of our warfare are not carnal but mighty in God for pulling down strongholds.

2 Corinthians 10:4 NKJV

Finally, be strong in the Lord and in his mighty power. Put on the full armor of God so that you can take your stand against the devil's schemes.

Ephesians 6:10-11 NIV

Having disarmed the powers and authorities, he made a public spectacle of them, triumphing over them by the cross.

Colossians 2:15 NIV

You are of God, little children, and have overcome them, because He who is in you is greater than he who is in the world.

1 John 4:4 NKJV

A bruised reed he will not break, and a smoldering wick he will not snuff out, till he leads justice to victory.

Matthew 12:20 NIV

Submit yourselves therefore to God.
Resist the devil, and he will flee from you.

James 4:7 KJV

With God we shall do valiantly; it is he who will tread down our foes.

Psalm 60:12 ESV

When the perishable has been clothed with the imperishable, and the mortal with immortality, then the saying that is written will come true: "Death has been swallowed up in victory." "Where, O death, is your victory? Where, O death, is your sting?" The sting of death is sin, and the power of sin is the law. But thanks be to God! He gives us the victory through our Lord Jesus Christ.

1 Corinthians 15:54-57 NIV

He holds victory in store for the upright.

Proverbs 2:7 NIV